DeMOCKracy

by Aaron Lang

RoseDog Books
PITTSBURGH, PENNSYLVANIA 15238

RoseDog Books
585 Alpha Drive, Suite 103
Pittsburgh, PA 15238
Visit our website at *www.rosedogbookstore.com*

ISBN: 978-1-63764-488-1
eISBN: 978-1-63764-537-6

DeMOCKracy

An exploration of the relationship between democracy, "necessary evils," corruption, and realpolitik.

"In the councils of government, we must guard against the acquisition of unwarranted influence, whether sought or unsought, by the military-industrial complex. The potential for the disastrous rise of misplaced power exists and will persist."

~ Excerpt from President Eisenhower's Farewell Address

Do you believe it to be true that "absolute power corrupts absolutely"? That adage is a sentence which, if aggressively analyzed, could force someone to think on it for a lifetime. The immediate response is questions, and an endless flow of them. What is power, and from where is power derived? Power, in a simple definition, can be called the ability to create change based on influence and/or might. Power can also be derived from severe need and extortion. Power can be, one might say, from exorbitant wealth, firepower, and technologies or even from political or ideological manipulations. Power does seem to be a fluid definition with subsequent equivocal levels. There are leaders, alliances, contracts, contingencies, insurgencies, coup d'états, and mutinies, which certainly cover an array of power struggles be they military or political, or a deadly fascist combination.

There are domestic and international common/civil/criminal laws, prisons, authorities, riots, protests, lobbyists, and abolitionists, all with various forms of power and influence. The same can be said of the sole possession of nuclear bombs, or of the influence of an institution like the US Federal Reserve. Power could be called electricity or the ability to spread one's voice to the world. In a globalized context, however, how could people ever achieve "absolute power"? From what basis of solidarity, or even divinity, do the powerful draw their resolve? What would you say is the "gold standard" for power? When thinking of "absolute power," one can hardly relieve themselves of a plethora of thoughts about the past and the stories of power from antiquity. Although there are many interconnected levels in the hierarchy of humanity's institutional powers, there is one source of power that is the literal foundation of all. The source of power which has always easily presented itself in the study of history, either as territory, resources, or loyal population, is *land.*

Most land throughout time has been, and now is perennially, owned by governments and corporations. In the modern context, the temporary owners of residences and small businesses are subject to foreclosures, evictions, and bankruptcy, with few prospects of reclaiming the areas of "ownership," because they do not have the collateral nor savings to in/ensure the revival and prosperity of the property. The median-level of businesses, such as wealthy chains of hotels found in major metropolises, or prestigious institutes of art and science, have many of the benefits of a macroscale conglomerate which will save the land's ownership. However, most businesses and landowners lack *conglomeration*: wealth from around the globe, based on the land being served somehow, and the backing and money of the people of the land, creating not only customer "security" and intimacy but also corporate power. Banks, oil magnates, food companies, and media conglomerates are arguably a small list of corporations that are at the macro level of power which hold the most sway of people's lives and are only kept "in check" by the offices of political authority. In the US, the federal power players come in the form of agencies such as, but not limited to, the FDA, SEC, EPA, FCC, FBI, DEA, CIA, ATF, DOJ, and DOD.

However, very often government agencies and law enforcement are on the side of business. Governments have the ability to withhold utilities, set limits on pricing, create special taxes, refuse admission to a Chamber of Commerce, investigate code violations, expropriate land, and make contracts with companies for development that the governmental body chooses. There are many levels to government, from local to federal, and they all have the ability to set reasonable standards for business and regulate the land they tax, by law, policy, or general administration.

The acquisition of land is nothing without people producing commodities, services for the people, and, importantly, taxes and an economy to regulate.

The modern global economy does have remnants of old trade routes and standards, but the majority of countries have been brought into a global economy by force, either physical force or desperate need to join the new systems in place. Empires like the British, or even the Spanish, were the beginning of a "modern" trend of using military to conquer or occupy a nation, and then business relationships will be created based on the workforce and resources available from the land. The people who live in the motherlands of empires also work fervently for the empire while constantly consuming its bounty and praising the illustrious leaders who brought it to them. This imperial tradition, which is as ancient as the Romans or Persians, did not stop with the US.

The US government after WWII, in its quest to end communism, became the dominant occupying force of many lands, through military and intelligence operations, and inserted its influence into these countries for business, resources, and guaranteed allies. The trend will be shown in this book that government and industry very often have the same interests, in foreign or domestic matters, with regard to expanding the sphere of influence of the US. Alliances, international trade organizations and treaties, and mutual benefit between two or more governments have dictated the global needs of maintaining power, order, and exorbitant profit margins, all while ignoring the many injustices caused in the US and around the planet.

Power, being the ability to make tangible or quantifiable change, must be rooted in the stakes which other power players will be "playing" against and/or with. The game of power is a game of conquest, and in our modern era, it is predicated on the pretense that the US (and its allies) must dominate the world, or "Communists" will—and if they take over the world, then it will be ruined. And our mission to stop them might just ruin it first. Perhaps that is hyperbole, but what is meant by "ruining" in this context is that the spending for international military and intelligence efforts, compounded with the physical ramifications of para/military operations, contributes to a global environment in which the US, and similar governments, have been allowed to act lawlessly. This is also true in international business. Not only does the military and intelligence spending waste a considerable amount of tax money that could be used for services to its people, but international business has set its sights on the whole world while leaving their fellow citizens behind.

At this point, for systemic solutions to many of the problems, which will be mentioned throughout this text, there is a need to adhere to international laws and standards for human rights while also consistently paying attention to the areas where domestic and international laws need to be updated based on the damages to, or needs of, a country's quality of life. Because what we have is a modern empire which has forced or coerced many nations in the world to ally itself to the military and business interests of the US for mutual benefit and safety from the "Communists." This has occurred with many international treaties, agreements, laws, and organizations like NATO. And, ironically, many times the "bad guys" are US allies.

This chapter's quote from Eisenhower, which discusses the "Military-Industrial Complex," is an indication of fear that a war-profiteering system, which is supply-and-demand based, could disintegrate prototypical "American values." This is a notion which a president offered, and which is a framework for understanding the Venn-Diagram of corporate and governmental needs. The Military-Industrial Complex has played itself out in many ways, which will be described throughout this text, but the Complex was the progenitor of an insidious brainchild that encompassed more than war-profiteering: modern Empire, or what will be coined in this book as the "Imperial-Industrial Complex." Eisenhower was a five-star general of the US military before becoming president, and he was aware that his country was a superpower after World War II, but he could not foresee that the US military and businesses would spread out to the corners of the Earth for an indefinite period of time.

The US government has been playing a "Game of Power" with Russia since 1945. And it is that point which is the driving force behind this book. The amount of history, scandal, conquering, espionage, counterinsurgency, and political suppression that is tied back to the notion of the US and the USSR competing is astounding. And throughout this text, we shall explore what that looks like historically, how it is played out in geopolitics, and why two global superpowers have used the nations of this planet as if they were a playground for claiming resources and keeping out the competition.

Naturally, resources are a main reason why land makes a nation so powerful. But what other machinations are at play? Is total domination the goal to ensure "the other guy" does not win? As we all know, governments and businesses, at almost any price, want access to precious metals, oil, food, fertile land, and everything in between. Empires of the past controlled many global resources before WWII, but afterward, these two "new kids on the block" started taking over the inherited, and disintegrating, properties of recently traumatized societies. Throughout this book, we shall explore the rationale and social psychology of "Anti-Communism" and "American Exceptionalism," from 1945 to 2020, to understand how state-corporate ambitions have focused on expanding and maintaining their sphere of influence while abandoning their country. This clash of ideologies, of democratic capitalism and communism, is still going on to this day, and it is an agenda that goes from the top down, military to individual, in every facet of US domestic and foreign policy.

In this book, the framework will encompass a factual basis for using an "Imperial-Industrial Complex" lens, mainly in the form of historical examples and facts about the vast networks of the US; historical literature reviews and case studies; Rules for the Game of Power and policy recommendations. The book is ended with an abstract analysis of politics in the US. Therefore, we will cover the basics of technocratic power structures (how to play) and their alleged intentions, symbioses (required partnerships), policies and malfeasance (rules and cheating), and social control (power over the people) in this fight to be the only superpower. Furthermore, throughout this book, there will be explorations into globalism, hegemony, and realpolitik, because the world is the oyster that offers the pearl of everlasting riches. Land and riches are the basic elements which create structures of power. And, naturally, keeping your enemy from land and riches can be just as important as acquiring them in a game like this.

The question of democracy, meaning that the people have a right to vote on what is done with the power at hand, is also central to this book. It is the author's postulation that even democracy itself is an opiate of the masses that has been sold by the Empire to us, and that our modern Empire will only give power and money to the governmental and corporate elite. But the people deserve to have their voices heard on the military and business endeavors, which affect everyone from the blue-collar to the white-collar workers. Most politicians are either a willing participant in this game, or they are blinded by the status quo, ambition, and domestic panic, and they cannot see other options than what the agenda dictates.

The Imperial-Industrial Complex will be compared to other empires, too, because the expansionist aspect of stretching your empire too far will cripple the homeland. If the laws, regulations, and priorities which uphold these structures of neo-colonization are changed, then perhaps systemic change can occur over time. The changes which need assessed are these: military/intelligence spending and rationale, international business laws for specifically precious re-sources, enforcing antitrust laws, and searching for economic justice in the tax-budget. These changes would benefit the majority of those oppressed by this imperial game of conquest—from the farmer in the US to the factory worker in Beijing. Hopefully politicians will look into some of the recommen-dations made in this book, or find better answers. The people deserve to know what has been happening on an international scale, and how it affects them; and these are stories which the news will not air, or have forgotten. On that note, how can the people petition their representatives to make the right moves if they are misinformed? Democracy can become a forthright system of our future, or it will remain the distraction in place while those with power use their well-honed sleight of hand to defy the wishes of the populace and attempt to make most of this planet a part of the "American Empire."

Chapter 1:

A Brief History of the Economies of Wealth and Power, or "How to Play"

"There is no document of civilization that is not at the same time a document of barbarism."
~ Walter Benjamin in his "Theses on the Philosophy of History"

As anyone knows, the government's ability to create and enforce laws, along with being the masters of legalized force, are the main forms of the government's legitimacy. The other main forms of governmental power are the ability to tax and audit anyone from the individual to a conglomerate. Corporations fulfill the needs of governmental organizations through contracts or via necessity, and this can create a partnership of power. However, there are some corporations that undoubtedly have their sway solely based on their product and/or sheer wealth. But where did this power come from, and what does this power mean in the day-to-day lives of people across the planet?

When it comes to the United States, it is no mystery how the modern country came to be. Several powers from Europe claimed the land as their own, regardless of the fact that societies lived in all of the Americas beforehand. The power which propelled the Europeans across the Atlantic to claim their "New World" was that of their kingdoms, which all were granted their power from the Vatican. The papacy was able to tax countries, crown kings, refuse funds, excommunicate royals, and enact martial law with the Vatican army from roughly 700 AD to nearly 1700 AD. Therefore, it was the last vestiges of the ancient expansionist empire, the Romans, which transferred its power to the European powers, who in turn transferred that expansion and power-mongering to the newly found continents.

The main concept Spain conveyed to the rest of Europe when its envoys came to and from the Americas was that the power to exceed the papacy would come from new land. From the land, an entity can create space for farming and commerce, reap the land of natural resources to trade and sell, and establish new forts for military development and wealth hoarding. Naturally, the European quest for gold and grandeur resulted in intercontinental trade and eventually the creation of several new nations. A network of wealth and power hubs, from resources to soldiers to gold, creates the *illusion* of absolute power and the *very real* systems and institutions of imperial colonialism.

After Spain, the British empire was the next regal body to colonize a large swath of the planet, with territories in North America and the Caribbean, Africa, India, China, and other regions. The British eventually instituted the industrial labor force to replace lost slave labor, and as the Spanish had done with tobacco and rum, products from around the world became part of a cycle of supply/demand, trade, exploitation, piracy, and the new trend of global business. As soon as the United States established itself as a child of the old world, but the harbinger of the new, it amalgamated every lesson learned from European history and put them into practice. For the past 150 years, the United States has used expansion, globalization, and neo-colonialism to create a status that has been coined "American Exceptionalism." We are beholden to no international standards: we make them, and break them. What is exceptional is the power to be the business leaders, political entrepreneurs, and police of the globe.

The Origins of the Oligarchic Republic in the US

Land was doled out to white members of the new colonies in the US, and was granted for pioneers and homesteaders as well. This is a clear chain which demonstrates that military might leads to new land, and hence new monies, resources, and services; and as well, it must be acknowledged that historically militaries have used slavery to continue building the empire(s). This is the natural way in which conquest creates civilization but how civilization can then in turn be corrupted by the conquest-mindset. And to the point about sovereign power: even if people owned land "outright," if they did not pay their taxes and dues, however, the US government could easily expropriate this land, and it would be within their legal abilities and rights. However, once the 19th century version of "too big to fail" came along, then also followed the challenge to the idea of the US government's "sovereignty."

The power to rival the US government, and control it with the precursors to lobbyists, came from the wills and pocketbooks of several tycoons, namely Vanderbilt, Rockefeller, JP Morgan, and Carnegie. Never before had any people in the US controlled so much wealth unless they were the collective federal government. And these men knew exactly what they wanted, and how to manipulate situations and politics with "the almighty dollar" as it would come to be known. However, it must be stated that the author is not an economist, and the argument over the (un)ethical ways in which the men achieved their wealth is irrelevant to the point that they had much power at their command (research *Robber Barons*). Moving into the 20th and 21st centuries, it will be displayed throughout this text the ways in which money, business, and politics intersect for the pursuit of power.

It is common knowledge that wealthy families have bought influence in the forms of politicians and legislation throughout US history, and even many bribe-accepting legislatures elected officials, instead of popular votes, until the end of the 19th century. In fact, votes were so literally bought in the 19th century that voters used carbon copies to take to the funders of these wealth-based elections to get their share for their vote. As well, women were not able to vote until 1920 (research *Women's Suffrage*). There are two successive presidents who had a major impact on modern Campaign Finance Laws and Anti-Trust Laws at the turn of the 19th century, going into the 20th century, and those two men were William McKinley Jr. And Theodore Roosevelt. With diametrically opposing views, and in the same era of change, these men would throw the US systems of power into a newly formed cage, which one could equate to an Escher.

William McKinley Jr. and Theodore Roosevelt
William McKinley Junior (WMJ) was the poster boy for all presidents who would succeed him. WMJ was supported by wealthy businessmen such as Mark Hanna, and his campaign featured posters, buttons, and front-porch slam sessions of policy and politicians. WMJ's election as 25th president in 1897 assured that the "Genius of the Gilded Age" would come to fruition as a semipermanent structure of industrial revolution. WMJ's platform was one of domestic protectionism, retaining the gold standard while refusing the ideology of "free

silver," and of expansion regarding Latin America and areas in the Pacific. Many of his written or supported laws were quite liberating for the US, including the McKinley and Dingley Tariffs and the Gold Standard Act, primarily because this meant that the US had ostensible leverage over bimetallist world powers. However, WMJ's favoritism toward the "1%" of the day was not unnoticed by the populace. In fact, McKinley won against William Jennings Bryan twice, whom the Rockefellers, Carnegies, Vanderbilts, and JP Morgan all wanted eliminated from the presidential race due to his populist leanings.

WMJ's presidency saw the swift beginning and end of the Spanish-American war, precipitated by Cuba's subjugation, and as a consequence, the US received Puerto Rico, Hawaii, Guam, the Philippines, and Cuba as its annexed principalities. Due to the newly installed tariffs, there was an increase in domestic economic growth—so WMJ's presidency was appearing as a swimming success. Unfortunately, many US citizens (mainly farmers and industrial workers and their allies) realized that a majority of the "new profits" was going to the tycoons who used gold's status against the common worker. Since silver had either been worthless, or had fluctuated in amounts of pathetic worth compared to gold, since the Civil War, the wealth that preceded the Gilded Age was worth little, and the interest to pay in on the gold standard was too much in the economic climate. Much gold was found in the Yukon and Australia; however, this did not keep prices, interest, or contempt down for very long. The citizenry was worried about accessing paper money for ease of use and prosperity. Due to the unrest regarding WMJ's expansionism, reliance on "economic innovation" in the form of the Gold Standard, decrying unions, keeping wages low, and allowing seven-day workweeks (compounded with global uprisings), WMJ was assassinated in 1901.

The vice president at the time, Theodore (Teddy) Roosevelt, then became the sitting president until an election could take place. Teddy became the official president and began "trust-busting," proposing to Congress that corporate donors should be outlawed entirely—while taking contributions from wealthy corporate "suits" like many others. However, Teddy may have simply been playing the game so that some advanced "refereeing" could take place in the future. Theodore Roosevelt took JP Morgan, James J. Hill, and their newly conglomerated Northern Securities Company (railroad empire) to court for violating the Sherman Antitrust Act of 1890 (ehistory.osu.edu).

Regarding the Supreme Court's decision:

> Neither Hill nor Morgan figured on Theodore Roosevelt and the power he was bringing to the presidency. Roosevelt's Department of Justice prosecuted the Northern Securities Company for violating the Sherman Act. In 1904, the Supreme Court agreed with the administration's position, and ordered the Northern Securities company dissolved. For Roosevelt, this proved a great victory. Not only did the victory earn him the politically popular title of 'trust buster.' The victory asserted the power of the presidency and demonstrated that the executive branch was even more powerful than the nation's most powerful business institutions. In the seven years he served as President, Roosevelt brought suit against 43 other trusts (ehistory.osu.edu).

One of those "43 other trusts" was Rockefeller's Standard Oil Company. Teddy was not messing around when it came to trusts, or what we today would call monopolies. Teddy was ready to combat some of the more corrupt elements which were forming in a modern America. This included business practices of buying out or destroying competition, building monopolies, and paying politicians and the citizenry for favorable politics. Most historians agree that effective Campaign Finance Law was not established in the US until the Tillman Act of 1907, which was approved by Teddy's administration. The Tillman Act was built upon by additions to it over a period of sixty years. Spending limits and donor disclosure were made mandatory for Congress by 1911. Then new bills were passed, such as The Federal Corrupt Practices Act of 1925 and the Hatch Act of 1939, which established fiscal limits like three million dollars for political parties' campaign expenditures and five thousand dollars for individual campaign contributions.

The schema of politicians being paid by *interested parties* or *demanding powers* is as old as the profession. However, if the Constitution of the United States of America was to be upheld in an ethical framework, which espouses the democratic process, there would need to be regulations for monetary contributions. Article III of the Constitution outlines traitorous and treasonous behavior on the part of foreign parties, but throughout the development of the nation, we will see how the laws of the land legitimize the entanglements of foreign governments, international business interests, and American politics in a way the Founders would have decried.

Naturally, the era of campaign finance and anti-trust laws was, in essence, about preserving the power of the people. As well, Teddy was a man with a vision for his country, and he was not as focused on expanding and becoming a superpower. Focus on the prosperity of the people of your country will almost always be coupled with economic fairness, ending costly expansionism, and having pride about national trends of production and innovation—not global trends. These two presidents offer insight into the two perspectives which the US struggles with to this day: keeping in mind either the best interests of American citizens or the best interests of an expansionist regime.

The Native Americans were killed in the beginnings of the European invasion of this land and, eventually, were forced onto the Trail of Tears or onto reservations of their own sovereign land. All treaties and promises taken into consideration, it was the white man who was the "Indian Giver," a term which clearly was used to justify racism, hate of the enemy, and an endless invasion full of hostility. Natives were seen as barbarians, and they needed "liberated." This topic, and nearly all justifications for expansionism and occupation, will be addressed throughout this book. As mentioned earlier, the era of WMJ and Teddy saw many battles with the Spanish, a contending empire which had laid claim to many of the lands in North and South America since the time of Cortez and other conquistadors.

It seems as if Teddy wanted to focus more on the needs of his people rather than the Treasury's need for gold or the military's need to extinguish Spanish influence. However, Teddy was involved in securing sections of Texas, Arizona, New Mexico, and California, after the events of the Alamo, because he believed those lands to be US property, not Mexico's. In reality, they always were Mexican (or Spanish) property in the past. But the point remains that Teddy did what he thought was best for his nation, and not what was best for business tycoons, generals who wanted glory in destroying the Spanish, or an agenda to ensure the Treasury could back up paper money with gold from around the world. Unfortunately, the laws and legal precedents which were established during the Teddy Administration have been easily circumvented in our modern times. Not only have these laws been circumvented, but new laws (or the elimination of old laws) have rendered the sentiments of the age of Teddy Roosevelt impotent, while glorifying the work of WMJ. Because the rationale of American polity has become a competition to "be the ultimate superpower, always expand our sphere of influence, and liberate the barbarian." We will tease out how this vague agenda is enacted from WWII to 2020 during the course of this text. (*To be continued in chapters 3 and 5.*)

Now that some of the most famous names and events from the beginning of the 20th century in the US have been mentioned and elaborated upon, it is quite striking that the scenarios and issues seem like the issues going on in 2020! Banks and corporations paying for politicians' ascent to the legislative, judicial, or executive branches of the US government, constant corruption scandals and policy amendments, and the ever-growing issue of American hegemony in the world and how it affects US citizens. Obviously, these precursors led to the Great Depression, which cannot be fully investigated in this monograph. However, the US was not the top world power until 1945—just a runner in the race—so, to understand how the same issues of the beginning of the 20th century are only exacerbated by the beginning of the 21st, the query must move to the World Wars and their after-effects on the US and the planet. The US political economy will be returned to, but the chronology of power is important. Under the current hypothesis, the most likely source of "absolute power" is going to come from *land*. Land is gained through military might and immense wealth—and remember to ask yourself, "Do I get a vote on war or international business in 2020?"

Chapter 2:

The World Tournament, or "The Big Game"

"It is the right of war for conquerors to treat those whom they have conquered according to their pleasure."

~ from Julius Caesar's "Comentarii de Bello Gallico"

World War Two (WWII) is one of the most discussed, analyzed, and theorized upon events in all of history, and regarding its recency, that is astounding and appalling. Therefore, WWII will not be addressed in a longform fashion in this book, but rather, its relationship to American Exceptionalism will be teased out of facts which are pertinent to this tale of "absolute power" and land-grabbing. One bit of common knowledge, which is a great place to start, is that the globe was fractured after WWII, and in reality, the globe as we know it today only exists because of the restructuring the League of Nations, later known as the United Nations (UN), mandated. Take these examples in mind: the Austro-Hungarian Empire was a reformed area which mixed portions of the Holy-Roman Empire and the Ottoman Empire (of which the rest was eventually reclaimed as "the Middle East"), Africa was a divided continent of colonies and original tribes, and the Japanese Empire ruled almost all of Asia—but all of that was dissolved between the years of the World Wars to circa 1960. Alas, the world saw an end to many old and new empires from the years of 1900 to 1945; however, one empire would emerge from all of this chaos to become the most powerful the world has ever seen.

The United States found the perfect way to become the world leader in 1945, and that way could be called the "Democratization of the World." The globe became a laboratory for empirical evidence of what would later be coined as the "Neoliberal" age—meaning that the "choice" of "freedom" and "democracy," which is "the only way" for the world to ostensibly progress, is to have laissez-faire capitalism backed by the militarily democratized countries. The first countries to become "democratized" in this era were technically Japan and Korea—countries which the US military occupied after winning wars against them, bringing in military bases and companies from "the first world." However, countries such as the Democratic Republic of the Congo had CIA agents (Frank Carlucci), and Chile had Chicago School sociologists (Milton Friedman), putting the will of the Imperial-Industrial Complex into play: for access to precious-metal mines in Africa and putting US business in South America (BBC, 2003; Klein, 2007; Rothe, 2009). (Case studies will be introduced later to delve into these topics.)

The experiment of neoliberal "democratization" has become akin to the concept of the Judeo-Christian God's notion of making humans in his image. Meaning that the world has become a playground of sorts to make "them" like "us." For example, the US has military bases in eighty countries around the world, yet there are no foreign military bases in the US—and this is by design (Slater, 2018). The design is one based on running the world with two basic types of power: hard and soft. Hard power being that of the military and police, and soft power being that of any type of influence—especially including law, industry, and media.

The term "superpower" came out of WWII just as the word "genocide" did. There are penultimate reasons for the creation and circulation of these terminologies, and it is because the world had never before seen such a depth of debauchery and destruction. And never before had the world needed heralds of unity and hope as it did in 1945. The US and the USSR were the top powers after democratic nations in Europe had either wrought destruction or been destroyed; however, there was a clear split in Eurasia: "democracy and capitalism" or "communism." The evils of Stalin were impossible to miss, just as Hitler's were, and the fear of a Gulag, or another Hitler, was too powerful to let "mediocre" or "disintegrated" nations fend for themselves. Thus, the reconstruction of the globe was to begin with the United Nations' three main prerogatives: remapping the former empires (taking into account existing structures), "fixing" the former colonies and territories with loans and "urbanization," and the Geneva Convention's International Humanitarian

Law (Laws of Armed Conflict) and International Human Rights Law (OHCHR,2020).

Along with new "rules of engagement," which mostly banned certain weapons from combat, came new territories for absorption. The USSR dominated Eurasia, covering a landmass that no "empire" before it had—albeit Siberia and neighboring areas are nigh uninhabitable. The USSR found its reach in eastern Europe generally, including Germany, and it had a grip on Asian countries which bordered US allies. The world, it seemed, had two colors, which could indicate the socio-political demography of the years 1945–1970: blue (US) and red (USSR). One major example that persists to this day is the Israeli-Palestinian conflict, because it was this era of reconstruction and US-backed "democratization" which established Israel in territory the Palestinians claimed. The process included making Israel an ally, and ensuring they were well protected with American weaponry and favor. The US was making sure to have a foothold near all areas which Russia was "friendly" with—this includes the US's strategic placement in Germany, Japan, Israel, Egypt, Chile, Nicaragua, and a long list of other, or eventual, military bases or covert operations (Macmillan, 2009; Slater, 2018).

The next level to follow hard power is soft power. The world wanted to either befriend the US and similar nations, or they wanted to root for the other team, which was the USSR. Many nations from Asia to South America were on the side of the USSR. However, the USSR became insulated and suspicious, whereas the US realized that "the game" had changed after 1945—classic "land-grabs" were not going to be the way to ingratiate cultures as ancient empires had done. The world was watching, and aside from the "skirmishes" being settled by a superpower, the world was tired of war.

Aside from military bases, the influence that the US needed was based on globalization. This influence can come in the form of loans, interest/repayment, and international industry, banking and media. This included Germany, who was going to be paying reparations for two World Wars, but it also included nations which were freed from subjugation or forced into the capitalistic system with a certain immediacy-mixed-with-shock factor (read Naomi Klein's *The Shock Doctrine*). This included newly freed African nations, nations which were in the borderlands of "red" and "blue," or any nation which officially wished to join the "First World." Japan was definitely incorporated into this new global economy by force, occupation, shock, and need. Japan became a booming economy eventually, but everything has not been peaches and cream. Japan will offer us a case study into the positive and negative effects of the project of "democratization," what Eisenhower was seeing in his time and the Imperial-Industrial Complex generally.

A Case Study on the Effects
of Military Occupation and Post-War Industry in Japan

Japanese industrialization has assisted them in becoming a top-tier economic power, and has given them the ability to sustain a thriving market, excellent diplomacy, and has made them one of the more charitable nations in the world. According to *Japan and America: Global Partners* by Yoichi Funabachi, a Tokyo-based diplomatic correspondent, "Japan could have never been a good loser if the United States had not been a good winner" (Funabachi, 1992). Japan, after WWII, was occupied by the US, who also aided in their reconstruction. The Japanese were demilitarized (and still are), their government was reconfigured into a parliamentary democracy, and they were made US trading partners. These transitions, along with the industrious spirit of the country, assisted Japan in becoming a $4.9 trillion GDP nation, but there have been some downsides.

Japan is an economic titan no doubt, but how many workers does it take to keep figures elevated? As of 2014, 65,870,000 of the 110,820,000 Japanese workers who are aged fifteen years old and over are part of the physical labor force, and 85 percent of Japan's population lives in urban areas, which account for only 3 percent of Japan's geography (everyculture.com; stat.go.jp). Unfortunately, the high-stress life of the industrial Japanese has been linked to Japan's high rate of suicide. As of 2012, Japan had the seventh highest rate of suicide per capita in the world (terrific-top10.com). Approximately thirty thousand people a year from 1998–2012 committed suicide, and amongst developed nations, Japan had the second highest rate below Russia (apecsec.org).

According to "Japan: Ending the Culture of the 'Honourable' Suicide," by Andrew Chambers of the *Guardian*, suicide is the leading cause of death for males in the age range of twenty to forty and females in the age range of fifteen to thirty-four (Chambers, 2010). There is a myriad of causes that include stress from work/finances, PTSD from the 2011 earthquake, life-insurance money for familial posterity, and miscellaneous unknown reasons (apecsec.com). So, the things that are causing these suicides seem to be related to stress: about money, about natural disasters, about work and family; the Japanese also do not necessarily have a "Western" taboo on suicide. Industrialization and capitalism have caused city workers to commit suicide due to the direct causes aforementioned, and a percentage of workers stated that they have depression, and that could be a cause as well. Another possibility is a societal identity crisis: a problem for Japan since the process of Westernization. As will be revealed below, the identity crisis is happening on many levels in Japan.

Japan is no stranger to European and American foreigners arriving on their shores and altering their way of life through force and coercion into the global market and hierarchies. Their identities have been "Westernizing" since the Spanish arrived in Asia, and definitely after Matthew Perry arrived from the US in the 1800s. In the modern context, the Japanese have been struggling with their place in capitalism and their purpose in life, and for the newest generations, they have become socially withdrawn. *Hikikomori* is a psychosocial disorder which has occurred in Japan, and it is similar to the Eurocentric diagnosis of "agoraphobia" (Dziesinski, 2004). The approximately one million *hikikomori*-afflicted are hermits, recluses, misanthropes, and are devoid of social interaction. They are usually unemployed, suffer from clinical diagnoses similar to anxiety and depression, and they only live out their identity in an online format (Dziesinski, 2004).

This next perspective displays how *hikikomori* is connected to Post-War Japan, just as globalized industrialization and suicide rates are. Below is a quote which demonstrates the struggle of the Japanese people during societal changes, which have been ongoing in Japan with no little part played by America:

In the essay 'Japan's Lost Generation' (2000) by novelist Murakami Ryu on the hikikomori issue, he argues that members of a society suffer from tremendous stress in their personal lives when the nation in which they live undergoes structural change. Murakami, who just recently published a novel called Symbiosis Worm featuring a hikikomori as the protagonist, posits that stresses caused by a person's social framework changing right under their feet is cause for the formation of unique types of neurosis such as hikikomori. Murakami states: In 19th -century Europe, doctors often diagnosed 'hysteria' as a neurosis (almost always applied to women) that indicated a suppressed desire for social fulfillment. Once it became common for women to leave the home and take up positions in society, this 'hysteria' became a rarity. Murakami believes that the great economic prosperity of post-war Japan and the technological boom of recent years has caused great shifts in Japanese societal structure; factors, incidentally, that are contributors to the hikikomori phenomenon…It is highly probable that the hikikomori phenomenon is not new at all but is a social symptom of Japanese Post-War society. A culture which places high social prestige upon education means that those with gifts or perspectives not recognized within the scope of the standardized educational system feel their only recourse is to withdraw as no other social route is currently offered to them (Dziesinski, 2004).

Japan has internalized the problems presented by the past and modern life, but not every culture is the same. In countries where this pattern of neo-colonization exists, there are also externalizing varieties of identity crisis or rebellion. Those potentials will be demonstrated in other case studies in this book, along with the different types of governmental corruption and human rights abuses. Japan has been an excellent trading partner, and a friend to the developed and developing world alike; however, their citizenry is feeling suppressed and depressed. Another reason for those things, which correlates with the purposes of this text, is that Japan has felt occupied since the end of WWII because US military presence has been there since that time. Japan feels punished and under the dominion of another sovereign nation, and therefore, their independence and culture are warped by American needs and culture. This is the trend of hard power resulting in the influences of soft power.

The Rest of the World, the UN, and the US after 1945

The UN handed out an invitation of global peace, and with that invitation, the US invited its presence into several nations as the newly formed International Monetary Fund (IMF) and the World Bank (WB) (imf.org). These entities are contracted with nations to give loans for infrastructure-development, reconstruction, or humanitarian aid; so, eventually, the aim is to build electrical grids and power companies, roads (if needed), dams and water treatment facilities, banks, schools, and other municipal amenities. These loans create a heavy toll of repayment, and the partnerships created have also caused unrest and corruption on many levels. So, even though the amenities are technologically advanced and of utility, there are many nations in which the people had lived a traditional lifestyle that had persevered for millennia. Many peoples have been thrust into a capitalistic lifestyle which changed such things as where people access their water, which crops they are allowed to grow, and what kind of jobs they are allowed to have, among other issues. This is all required by the industries, banks, and governments of "democratizing," loan-shark nations. The World Trade Organization is another Post-WWII economic regulator for modern imperialism (and one which we will explore in the next chapter).

Along with "world peace," but more related to the Geneva Conventions than the International Monetary Fund, is the Rome Statute. The Rome Statute of the International Criminal Court (ICC) of 2002, which gave an international body the right to prosecute leaders of nations for war crimes or crimes against humanity, has not been ratified by the United States (umn.edu). There are two main reasons that the US has not ratified the Rome Statute: 1) the US is the "peacekeeper" of the world, ostensibly, and US leaders feared retaliation by other countries in an international setting, and 2) the US considers itself ultra-sovereign, exceptional and beyond the prosecutorial jurisdiction of an international court (Lederer, 2018). Simply meaning, US presidents and vice presidents are exempt from international prosecution for various crimes which will be mentioned throughout this text.

The US has ratified many treaties: The International Covenant on Civil and Political Rights, the Protocol Amending Slavery Convention, the Abolition of Forced Labor Convention, the International Convention on the Elimination of All Forms of Racial Discrimination, the Convention against Torture and Other Cruel, Inhuman or Degrading Treatment or Punishment, and the Convention on the Prevention and Punishment of the Crime of Genocide (umn.edu). The United States has not ratified one treaty regarding women's rights, union rights of workers (Freedom of Association), educational rights, or refugee/asylum rights (umn.edu).

The United States ratified all terrorism-related treaties, and naturally, all of the main Laws of Armed Conflict which were part of the Geneva Conventions after WWII and the Nuremberg Trials. However, even if the US violates the Geneva Conventions, the US has not ratified the Rome Statute and cannot be prosecuted when international crimes occur, or when a ratified treaty is violated. For example, the well-documented torture of people incarcerated at Guantanamo Bay, and many elements of the Iraq War, have been noted as violations of international law. As well, there are many ways of getting around the laws of international human rights—such as freeports for minerals/metals mined by slaves of warlords, offshoring work to "leniently" regulated countries, bank accounts and shell companies in the British Virgin Islands, secret meetings, refusal to extradite parties involved in crimes overseas, or flat-out denials of wrongdoing.

This is where the mindset of conquest has gotten both power hungry and paranoid, like with Caligula or Nero in the Roman Empire, and has allowed the few elite in government, military, and business to act with impunity since they believe they are above the law and everything they do is for the betterment of humankind. While incidentally inflating their bank accounts and egos to such extents that the only people in the 99 percent who could relate are those with the truest forms of narcissism and sociopathy. In modernity, this conquest for land and control began as World Wars, and the recuperation from them, but it has become a system of oppression all around the globe. Therefore, it seems as if we have explored the logic of the Imperial-Industrial Complex from its infancy to more mature development. From this point on, the global stage of political theatre will allow us to investigate the international intersections of US trade and business, which will then lend insight into the political and economic problems of solely the United States. The "Rules of the Game of Power" will also be introduced.

Chapter 3:

The Symbiotic Relationships
of Globalization, Government, and Industry

"For we are opposed around the world by a monolithic and ruthless conspiracy that relies primarily on covert means for expanding its sphere of influence—on infiltration instead of invasion, on subversion instead of elections, on intimidation instead of free choice, on guerrillas by night instead of armies by day. It is a system which has conscripted vast human and material resources into the building of a tightly knit, highly efficient machine that combines military, diplomatic, intelligence, economic, scientific and political operations. Its preparations are concealed, not published. Its mistakes are buried, not headlined. Its dissenters are silenced, not praised. No expenditure is questioned, no rumor is printed, no secret is revealed."

~ An Excerpt from President John F. Kennedy's Address
to the American Newspaper Publishers Association

Have you ever heard someone say "Well, that's just the way it is" or "That's just the nature of the world"? These are cognitive tools which allow one to detach from thoughts of problems beyond our own personal control, and the phrases allow for a simple order which exists as "solidly" as the Earth. As well, the adage "the more things change, the more they stay the same" may be true, but denial of realities and responsibilities are the projection of egoism which comes from a standpoint of privilege. There is a whole globe, which seems connected and struggling together, but the world does not struggle equally, and entire continents have been abused for centuries to the point that modern scientists claim that observable trauma can be passed down through DNA. Are advances allowable if they are made "on the backs," and sometimes by the death, of those who do not even have access to the products they manifest? How often do the common people in "democratic" nations get a vote on such things as international business (and exploitation)? And how often are they even informed on what is happening with regard to war in the world, business in the world, and how the Imperial-Industrial Complex affects them and they it?

When one thinks about having "a voice" in the political theater, they most likely think about their vote, or perhaps their social media presence, or a protest in which they participated. However, unless you are a politician, what exactly can the general citizenry vote on? Usually, votes are used to elect officials, and then those people vote on the issues and policies for a group of people, hence the term *representative*. They are literally meant to represent "the people," on their behalf, in official government matters. Otherwise, people typically get a vote on local tax measures and governmental projects, but is there really much else? What kind of a voice do you have if you can only impact tiny things in the grand scheme, unless one chooses to be a politician? A canary in a coal mine? Or, after considering the amount of influence lobbyists have, a canary in a tornado?

Polls taken around the nation show how the US feels on national issues. These polls are taken by Gallup, Pew, Bloomberg, Breitbart (Insert Thinktank or Newspaper's Name Here). However, these polls are opinions of the people (vox populi), not true votes. They always paint a picture of the US that looks so optimistic and open-minded; however, those are never the directions towards which policy turns its head. As it is with human beings, usually trauma or immediate shock make people change more than something which seems unconvincing from a source they will remain skeptical of due to biases and upbringing.

Therefore, the typical self-entrenching stances of the two-party political system in the US will never make the changes that are *necessary* for the progress of humankind based on prevailing extant evidence. This would require impartial and unbiased legislatures, which would require a change in framework and common goals in the US. If the US decided to make new Amendments to the Constitution, or new federal laws, and comply with international law, there could be systematic change. After this chapter there will be solutions proposed to almost every problem discussed, usually in the form of policy recommendations.

Until chapter seven, we will dive into nuanced topics of American Empire: from overall agendas, military action, and covert operations to transnational business, international law, and the society and politics of the United States.

Necessary Evils and the World Trade Organization

Now that some framework has been established, and some of the mirroring of the past has been discussed, we can look at some of the ways in which a modern empire ensures trading and profits. Achieving great wealth for an empire has always been a goal, to keep it in prosperity. And some say money is the root of all evil. But what are the necessary evils that a modern empire finds "permissible"? Perhaps it is military misconduct, tobacco and oil companies' awareness of deaths they indirectly cause, or the positive effects of Round-Up weedkiller outweighing the negative effects. Or perhaps it is laissez-faire capitalism which has allowed certain mega-corporations and banks to consolidate and defy anti-trust laws, oppress an international workforce, as well as influence politicians to create laws on their behalf or "look the other way." We are, after all, in the era of "too big to fail" and "too small to succeed," which was clearly demonstrated in the government bailout of all banks and parties involved in the 2008 economic crash of predatory loans and corrupt practices.

The World Trade Organization (WTO) is one group which internationally codifies the rationale of corporate greed while simultaneously exacerbating inequalities in developed and developing countries alike. The predecessor to the WTO was the General Agreement on Tariffs and Trade (GATT), which went along with Post-WWII reconstruction goals. By 1994 the "Uruguay Round Agreements" had been reached, which established the WTO, and many nations were now trading partners under a unified code. The WTO became a modern extension of a globalist mindset which allows almost anything to ensure "good" international trade.

Companies battle one another about products in the WTO, because for a country to enjoy participation in trade with the "big spenders," there cannot be regulations from one country which impede another country's ability to trade (Wallach and Sforza, 1999). Such as bans on lead, bans on beef hormones, bans on goods made with child or forced labor, bans on fishing methods, bans on gasoline contaminants, and many more unilateral "bans on bans." When countries tried to put these bans in place, opposing governments would threaten sanctions or WTO complaints, which would result in an international ruling. The rulings could be fines, allowable tariffs, or discontinuation of trade for a specific product with many countries.

This type of corporate-friendly regulation allows a company to say consumer and environmental safeguards are unfair business practices, all in the name of free trade. It can also mean the disenfranchisement of entire civilizations via patenting items which, before this era, were not able to be patented (GMOs of indigenous grains); ruining staple corn production in NAFTA countries (like Mexico); or making false promises to US citizens of cutting the trade deficit, raising median income, and providing excellent jobs for the blue- and white-collar workers alike (Wallach and Sforza, 1999). The opposite of promises made to the US population occurred after the Uruguay Round Agreements Compliance Act of 1998 became US law (Wallach and Sforza, 1999).

The Uruguay Round Agreements Compliance Act was created to ensure US companies and authorities complied with the new WTO, and to use the power of the pen to punish those who were not participating in global trade the way the US wanted them to. There are many examples of companies contributing to political parties to win favorable WTO outcomes; however, there is one interesting company which helped kickstart trends at the WTO: Chiquita. Yes, the banana company. Bananas do not seem that important, right? They are a great fruit that the world over enjoys, but they do not factor into your concept of power in the world most likely. In fact, this quote from Wallach and Sforza's (1999) "Whose Trade Organization?" displays exactly how easily politicians are bribed (and the resulting policies are usually much worse than the payoff):

> that governments with no economic stake, if the price were right, might be willing to do the bidding of multinational firms has aroused suspicions that the WTO dispute resolution system can be used on a 'rent-a-nation' basis. The Clinton administration filed a WTO complaint on bananas- a crop the U.S. does not grow for export- days after the U.S.-based multinational Chiquita gave $500,000 to the Democratic Party. Then...GOP Senate leaders introduced the 'Uruguay Round Agreements Compliance Act of 1998,' which imposed tariffs on the EU for not fully complying with the WTO. This move came one month after Chiquita CEO Carl Lindner donated $350,000-this time to the Republican Party.

We all know that donations to political parties, from oil conglomerates, billionaire philanthropists, or banana companies, result in policies which lend favor to the industry in question. Industries usually enjoy for regulations to be least restrictive, allowing for low pay to workers, low accountability regarding malfeasance, low standards for investigation (of facilities, of employees, and of financial records). These practices ensure that business progress for the health and safety of humankind is not achieved but also continues the cycle of business running government by proxy. Not only do these practices have legitimacy, even through third parties like Super PACs, they are also a microcosm of how the American Empire runs other governments by proxy. The Imperial-Industrial Complex focuses its ability to occupy as friend, or foe, on two pressure points: ongoing conflicts and trade potential.

The US has been considered the peacekeeper of the world since WWII, and with that title, they have decided which areas deserve attention/protection and which do not, and which countries are going to become our trading partners. US military bases and covert operations ensure that all knowledge is being passed to the appropriate authorities who will take political and militant action based on global trends (such as lumber, metal, food, medicine, weapons, oil, and so on). As well, the US having so many military bases and agreements ensures that certain nations cannot have a foothold in the global economy based on despotism or illegitimacy, such as trade restrictions on North Korea or Iran, until they comply with the international standards. Ironically, the US will sell weapons to, train soldier police of, and become business partners with despots—they just need to be an ally with great resources.

There have been several instances of the US being a 20th century petty tyrant. The obvious place to start is the literal overkill of the nuclear bombs used on Japan, which led to an occupation and lively business relationship. However, not even Germany was dealt such a devastating blow, but they had to comply with the Marshall Plan. Aside from direct military force, there is also a sufficient amount of covert operations which have established the US as the guiding force in a foreign territory. The assassination of Democratic Republic of the Congo leadership for access to mines (see below case study), Nicaraguan coups (Iran-Contra Affair), and Hussein's Iraq were largely CIA activity followed by business interests entering the area (Dobbs, 2002; Exoo, 2010; History, 2020; Morphonios, 2014). (*See chapter six for a detailed analysis of America's involvement in Iraq and the Iran-Contra Affair.*)

In the above instances, puppet governments were installed for access to mines, crude oil, iron ore, and poppy plants, among other commodities. As well, there was an undying goal of "ending" communism in the countries listed in the above paragraph. Then we have the "business as usual" instead of paramilitary, brand of occupation, offshoring production generally, and in deals like the North Atlantic Free Trade Agreement (NAFTA) and the Trans-Pacific Partnership (TPP). The globalization of labor to China and Mexico has created a legal system of criminally low wages and safety/health expectations for the workers, who can be underage, while simultaneously eliminating well-paid job opportunities for adult US citizens. In fact, a Chinese worker is typically paid less than one-tenth of what a US employee would make in the same position (Kavoussi, 2017). A mix of these occupations can be seen in the Congo.

The Democratic Republic of the Congo Case Study

This case study will help display the modern trends of globalization but also give the first of many examples in this book which demonstrate how the CIA and US businesses are vital organs of the Imperial-Industrial Complex. The Democratic Republic of the Congo (DRC) has had its fair share of colonization before the 20th and 21st centuries, and some of the dysfunction seen in the country will be derived from that or social disintegration. However, a greed for the wealth of that land, compounded with a desire to only use the resources instead of rule the nation, has created a human rights catastrophe based on purely financial and material needs of "developed nations." So, for the purposes of this book, the story begins not long after Congo was given its independence from Belgium after WWII.

In 1960 Patrice Lumumba was elected the first prime minister of the Congo (BBC, 2015). Lumumba solicited help from the USSR to avoid secessions and rebellions, and this was his "sudden death" one-strike failure which landed him in prison, and subsequently, he was assassinated by Frank Carlucci of the CIA with direct orders from President Eisenhower (BBC, 2003; Rothe, 2009). Carlucci was assisted by President Vubu and his chief of staff Joseph Mobutu, and this transpired due to the hopes of exhuming communism entirely from the people of the Congo. There have been multiple coup d'états and politicides within the DRC, and a full chronicling is beyond the scope of this text. Unfortunately, before the First and Second Congolese Wars (1996/1998), the country's history was already full of bloodshed and upheaval. The wars of the 1990s are what truly began the DRC's turmoil in late modernity (BBC, 2015; Ismi, 2014; Leader, 2008; OHCHR, 2010; Rothe and Mullins, 2008).

Uganda and Rwanda invaded the DRC in 1996, deposing Mobutu Sese Seko and installing Laurent Kabila as the de facto leader (BBC, 2015). The Wars were generally understood as a "revenge-genocide" in response to the Rwandan genocide (Ismi, 2014; Leader, 2008; Rothe and Mullins, 2008). The fighting through the Wars lasted into 2004, past the official end date of the second war, with approximately 3.8 million dead, having incurred genocide, mass murder, rape en masse, torture, disease proliferation, mass displacement (>2.4 million), and mass malnutrition (approx.16 million), thus being the largest loss of civilians in war since World War II (Leader, 2008; Rothe and Mullins, 2008). The DRC, a country which is worth twenty-four trillion dollars in minerals alone, is one of the poorest and most anomic societies in the world (Global Witness, 2014; Ismi, 2014; Leader, 2008; Rothe and Mullins, 2008).

After the Lusaka peace agreement of 1999 was enacted, Rwanda and Uganda officially decamped the DRC, but Uganda and Rwanda made excellent proxies, in the form of militias, to carry out their goals (Rothe and Mullins, 2008). Their goals mainly consisted of excavating as many precious resources from the land, and in ways that violate many laws. From 1995–2002, Uganda plundered over two hundred million dollars of gold from the DRC. The measurement of Rwanda's, Uganda's, and transnational corporations' guilt is twofold, being both fiscal and humanitarian. (1) The national export of gold versus national production of gold in Uganda is one excellent example of thievery and exploitation, which in 1999 was a shocking 11.45 tons of gold exported from Uganda, yet only .0092 tons were produced there (Rothe and Mullins, 2008). Similarly, Rwanda made roughly one million dollars per year between 1997 and 2000 for diamonds, yet Rwanda is devoid of naturally occurring diamonds (Rothe and Mullins, 2008). Clearly, metal and diamonds are being plundered out of the DRC. (2) Corporations in Uganda, Rwanda, and the DRC pay militias to mine metals and diamonds for them, and hence, the corporations continue the atrocities of war and slave labor so they may obtain these precious resources (Global Witness, 2014; Ismi, 2014; Leader, 2008; Rothe and Mullins, 2008).

The international market circumvents international economic and humanitarian/human rights laws (IHL/IHRL) quite easily, through "plausible" deniability and the leniency of the law via unrestricted market conditions in freeports in Switzerland; through the privileged secrecy of off-shore accounts and companies in the British Virgin Islands; *vis-à-vis* international ties of companies like Banro Gold, Casa Mining, Randgold, Mwana Africa, Loncor, Anglo-Gold Ashanti, Kilo Gold, Moku Gold, and many more—which are all US, Canadian, Australian, and European mining companies connected to Uganda and Rwanda (Brummer et al., 2012; Ismi, 2014; Rothe and Mullins, 2008). The DRC, due to corruption from within and without, has lost billions upon billions of dollars in potential revenue for the country for the sole benefit of a few elite (Ismi, 2014; Leader, 2008; Rothe and Mullins, 2008).

One person who most definitely fits the profile of an international elite businessman who furthers the agenda of the US is Dan Gertler. Dan Gertler is an Israeli billionaire, who is personal friends with the leaders of the DRC. He is known as the Gatekeeper to the mines in the DRC, owning most of the rights due to illegitimate and corrupt deals. With Israel's status of super-ally to the US, Gertler is "in the know" about business needs and international markets, and he continues to be in communication with officials from militias and the US government. Dan Gertler's first friend in the US government was Condoleeza Rice, and rest assured, he is in contact with the State Department to this very day. Gertler continues to make money from allowing this network of mining companies to have access to his mines, and allowing the slave labor of militias to be the ants who work for their queens.

Gold and diamonds were used in the examples above, but they are not the only valuable minerals which are brutally pilfered by militias from the DRC; three examples are coltan, cobalt, and copper. There are estimates that an amount of six million dollars of conflict minerals are smuggled out of the DRC daily (Ismi, 2014). The virulence and prominence of the militias which run certain areas of the DRC are not to be underestimated. There are more than forty such militias which have killed millions more since the 2004 war-statistic of approximately 3.8 million dead (up to 7 million total), have raped 400,000+ women, and have inducted more than 7,000 child soldiers (Free the Slaves, 2011; Ismi, 2014; Leader, 2008). The list is extensive, but three important factions are the Lord's Resistance Army (LRA), Rwanda Patriotic Front (RPF), and the, ostensibly, recently defeated M-23 (Ismi, 2014;

OHCHR, 2010; Rothe and Mullins, 2008). The only force which can penetrate this area legally is the United Nations (UN), and to date, their mini occupation has been ineffective.

The UN has been stationed, in either dormant or active phases, in the DRC since 1996. Their job is/was to rescue and rehabilitate victims of warfare, ward off the militias, and keep the peace, hence the name of their forces is Peacekeepers. After the Lusaka peace resolution was reached, the UN investigated illegal exploitation of miners in the DRC in 2000, and by 2002 they released a list of twenty-nine companies and fifty-four individuals which/who should be banned from the country through a legal apparatus (Leader, 2008). Furthermore, eighty-five companies, mostly Western, violated the Organization for Economic Cooperation and Development (OECD) guidelines for Multinational Enterprises (Leader, 2008). In 2010 the UN Office of the High Commissioner released a comprehensive mapping of massive amounts of human rights violations and crimes against humanity committed from 1993–2003 in the DRC and, shortly thereafter, created the United Nations Organization Stabilization Mission in the DRC (MONUSCO), which allotted approximately twenty thousand military or paramilitary personnel for further peacekeeping operations in the DRC (OHCHR, 2010).

The UN has not done very much in the DRC. In fact, they have created other paramilitaries which can be the "eyes and ears" of the governments involved in this corruption. Everything is not all bleak, but there will need to be so much work done to help the Congo. First of all will be the cessation of hostilities there, including cutting off the incentive corporations give to the occupying militias. The second will be strict business laws which are enforced. In the US, recent attempts have been made to ensure that business activities with an obvious "conflict minerals" chain of custody are stymied.

The Dodd Frank Act of 2010, or the conflict minerals law, required companies to submit their first report on the state of their minerals, and the chain of custody, by 2014. Global Witness and Amnesty International analyzed the companies' reports, from Apple, to Boeing and Tiffany and Co., and found that nearly 80 percent of the companies analyzed failed to meet the minimum requirements per the Act (Global Witness, 2015). In the Global Witness (2015) report, it is noted that the reason for this malfeasance was either due to blatant corruption or general business-like apathy about the minerals' origins.

In the US, though, corporations are rarely held accountable for complicity with, or participation in, crime. So, companies will be able to continue their deals through a vast, secretive, and ever-changing network of mining companies who are funding the figurative and literal rape of the Congo. All of this is in violation of several treaties which have been ratified by the US. However, the US would have to act on its own citizens who are, frankly, making too much money to prosecute. Or actual Mens Rea (intent) and Actus Rea (the act) of violating these international treaties would be difficult to prove by design. As well, regarding the Rome Statute, the US envisions itself above international law from the top down.

The New Game's Rules

What has happened in the DRC has happened in several nations. Military conquests, and then subsequent control of the land via hard and/or soft power, leads to governmental and corporate malfeasance. In the instance of the Congo, corporations pay militias handsomely to continue atrocities in the nation for profit from diamonds and metals. The metals are conductors, transmitters, and battery elements for iPhones, laptops, televisions, radio towers, electric lines, and a litany of other applications. In Chile and Nicaragua, their revolutionary leaders were part of plots to integrate those nations into the US Imperial-Industrial Complex. In Japan and Korea, the US was the direct military force to apply this pressure. The list goes on and on, and, once you see it, you will never miss the pattern of corporations infiltrating nations as soft power after hard power. Sometimes, soft power is all that is needed. We will explore this phenomenon throughout the entire book.

Nearly every country on the planet is dependent on the US and/or the UN and/or the WTO, which, in a nutshell, is hegemony. The US helped create the UN (and is the largest fiscal contributor) and, due to clever non-ratifications, will never be prosecuted for international violations of human rights or humanitarian law. The US created the GATT, which was the father of the WTO. The WTO upholds the flawed, unregulated practices of free trade which are upheld by international business laws and covert operations. The laws of the US are created by politicians who have been given a donation by an interested party, and that interested party is primarily interested in making as much money as possible regardless of human rights. The sectors of Defense and Intelligence do the bidding of upper-level officials in the Pentagon and White House—who all have a vested interest in the US being the "bread-winner" of the globe. This is Neo-Colonization systematized, and no average US citizen had a true vote on any of the matters mentioned in the past two chapters.

After all of this analysis, some Rules can now be stated for this Game of Power:

<u>Rule #1</u>: Have the hard power (military/police) and soft power (cultural influence and laws) to own land, tax the people, and generate immense amounts of work and trade.

<u>Rule #2</u>: Use international trade and influence to have at least soft power over the lands you do not have hard power over.

<u>Rule #3</u>: Utilize the power of "the power of the people," which entices citizens to be a part of the large matrix of the "Imperial-Industrial Complex"—in every country in which you have hard and soft power.

<u>Rule #4</u>: Create regulatory bodies (regulatory agencies, courts, councils for treaties) and force everyone to follow the same rules of engagement.

<u>Rule #5</u>: Capitalize and Avoid Taxation, Fines, and Prosecution

So, the game's rules are similar to the morphed golden rule: "He who has the gold makes the rules." Money can surely be a root of evil, and gold and imperialism go hand-in-hand. This is one of the more cynical yet realistic points about the state-corporate will of the United States as it relates to foreign and domestic policies. Solutions will be proposed in the next few chapters, but these problems (and more) must be illuminated first. We will continue our foray into world powers, but for a couple of chapters, we will dive into the belly of the beast. A lie has been told to the world, and one thing we have to start doing is tell the truth—from the inside, and out. As Exoo (2010) noted:

> No, America is not El Dorado. The Lone Superpower is not the Lone Ranger, righting wrongs wherever it goes. Capitalist hegemony and its monotonous story have not made ours 'the best of all possible worlds.' And yet, somehow, the alchemy of our mass media has made it seem so: It has made the land of inequality, the land of opportunity; the stench of belligerence, the bouquet of idealism; cupidity and rapacity, the American Way... [a] transformation of 21st-century American imperialism into the story of a benevolent America.

Chapter 4:

The "Rust Belt," Reaganomics,
and the Red Dragon, or Failed Expansion

"Government's view of the economy could be summed up in a few short phrases: If it moves, tax it. If it keeps moving, regulate it. And if it stops moving, subsidize it."

~ President Ronald Reagan

How do the Rules of the Game of Power affect you? Not only do you not get a vote on war, but you also do not get to vote on international corporate law, international trade deals (like NAFTA), or Department of Labor, IRS, or SEC guidelines. So, the rules affect the type of job you can obtain in a certain area, how well the wealth is or is not distributed amongst a company, the fact that many occupations have been shipped overseas to minimize payment to laborers, and the largest corporations in the United States barely pay income tax. On top of that, the company you do work for does not have to pay you a living wage, the national debt continues to rise, and you don't get one word in edgewise. Sounds fair enough, right?

Many economists and members of Congress have posited anecdotes that are similar to the one I will put in front of you now. If I am a McDonald's employee in New York City, and I make $8.00 an hour (which is over the federal minimum wage requirement of $7.25/hour), and I get forty hours a week, then I will make $320.00 a week before taxes and benefits are taken out. Once taxes and benefits are taken out of that gross income of $1280.00 a month, we can say that the person may take home around

$900.00 that month. In NYC, the baseline rent/mortgage cost is going to be $700–$1000 a month.

Already, that is not a living wage if a person is independent and has no roommates. Yes, there are ways to work around this fiscal quagmire, like roommates and another job, but people are regularly living at or below the poverty line while working in essential industries. As well, McDonald's is a multibillion-dollar company which could easily be more equitable to its employees. And I am talking about a company which has kept its workforce in the United States but is also transnational. Other companies have made a more devastating impact by globalizing their workforce and removing US factories and hubs which used to be the lifeblood of the blue-collar worker.

This all started in the 1970s, when many companies saw strikes and union debacles, let alone all of the hostile political atmosphere about the Vietnam War. It was a revolutionary powder-keg in its own right. The people were furious about conditions at home and abroad. By the 1980s, after many lay-offs and furloughs, factory and plant shutdowns, the mega-companies moved overseas to diversify their interests and minimize their wages. These could include, but are not limited to, DuPont, Ford, Proctor & Gamble, Chrysler, Kodak, 3M, Walmart, Carrier, Honeywell, GM, Nike, and a litany of other corporations. Thus, the term "Rust Belt" was born. The term implies that where once there was a mighty iron city of production, there is now a rusty husk of forgotten glory days. The academics would call eras like 1980–2000 "Post-Industrial," recognizing the inevitable ebb and flow of business. The current era is called the fourth industrial revolution; but we will get to that soon enough.

Ronald Reagan, the beloved president of the 1980s, has become a scapegoat for economic issues which originate in that decade. Reagan was a Republican whom the people felt they could count on, a champion of the masses. However, Reagan has been exposed to be as much of a morally neutral, demagogic image-monger as any person who has occupied the Oval Office since Nixon. Reagan did not truly have the interests of the US "everyman" at heart. But Reagan only allowed what Congress, the Senate, and large corporations wanted. Reagan did not try to force companies to produce in the US, he just went with the tide of globalization. Reagan also complained about government overspending, but the only tax reallocations, or government spending, he liked were for intelligence agencies to support rebels in foreign countries and for police to become paramilitary units (See chapters six and seven).

However, the 1970s were tumultuous to a degree, and Reagan was trying out one solution: Reaganomics. Economists have coined the term "Reaganomics" to connotate a specific brand of economics, which is called "trickle-down economics." Trickle-down economics is a concept which espouses a central belief: give CEOs and businessowners a majority of the funds, through deregulation and tax cuts, and it will be given to the workers in bonuses and wage increases, and to the community in charitable donations. As with many theories of social order or economics, this one fails in practice for a variety of reasons. When it comes to giving the majority of workers better wages, Reaganomics failed on that account more than any other. The main reasons are what you would expect: human and corporate greed.

An investigation into salaries and wages from the 1950s until today demonstrates that company profits were judiciously doled out after WWII. The lion's share of profits went to the large number of workers in the form of a living wage, and the CEOs or owners received more money for their leadership and innovation, but it was not an egregious amount which afforded the average worker unlivable compensation. In 1950 the average CEO made 20-to-1 what the average worker made, and today that number has multiplied by ten. In 2013 it was found that Fortune 500 companies' CEOs made on average 204-to-1 what their average employees made (huffpost.com).

Those numbers increased every decade, and their gold-lust was truly incentivized by the 1980s. The worker bees are not seeing their fair share of dividends that Mr. Reagan and all of his friends promised. In 2016 the average US household had $8,863 in their bank account according to data from the Federal Reserve (Martin, 2019). In that study, it was shown that people under thirty-five have less than the average, ranging from $1,300 to $4,000, approximately, based on marriage and childbearing status. As well, the Federal Reserve relied on a survey, which has its own methodological problems of omission/selectivity and will never reveal the financial situation of those without a bank account.

Related to flawed numbers is the unemployment rate. Since the Great Depression, which is the highest point on the line graph of US unemployment, unemployment rates have risen and fallen like waves. After WWII the unemployment rate was almost nonexistent for a multitude of reasons; after the economic problems of the 1970s and early 1980s, it reached nearly 10 percent; it fell again until a spike after the 2008 recession, and then reduced until the recent events of the coronavirus pandemic (which must be seen as an outlier) (Amadeo, 2020a). However, unemployment rates only track those who are receiving benefits from Department of Labor Unemployment funds, which is a great safety network akin to Medicaid/Medicare and Health and Human Services Welfare Funds for vulnerable populations, but it does not track those who do not file for unemployment nor those who live a low-quality life due to income. In 2018 "the Census Bureau found that 38.1 million people were poor...about one in eight Americans still lived below the poverty line — $25,465 for a family with two adults and two children" (Fessler, 2019).

Some of the blame has to be placed on corporations which have systematically offshored jobs to other countries, which directly oppresses people in other countries and indirectly oppresses US citizens. US citizens often cannot find quality blue-collar jobs which will provide a living wage, benefits, and an increased quality of life. Furthermore, this vulnerability of poverty is correlated with mental health disorders, substance abuse, and criminal activity like gang involvement, trafficking dangerous drugs, trafficking family members for commercial sex, robbery/burglary/theft, and general fraud or tax fraud (Goffman, 1963; Hagedorn, 2008; Maruna, 2000; Potter, 1994; Simon et al, 2018).

So, why did the corporations decide to send a majority of their labor to China, Japan, and Mexico and never look back? There are a few incentives:

1) The federal reserve and the treasury department were encouraging companies to offshore production because certain countries (China, Japan, UK, Luxembourg, Brazil, etc.) bought Treasury notes or get paid in Treasury notes for their exports/business (Amadeo, 2020b; Beltran et al, 2012). This means that those countries share in our debt because they have a stake in our economy, and if the economy does well, then they receive interest on their bond(s)/note(s). Which means, in the future, these countries could liquidate their assets and receive more money than they put in; or these countries are eligible for loans and assistance from the US while being a shareholder of the federal bank.

2) The old "capitalist paradox" manifested is this: you must go into debt to make money. In particular, countries like China needed to boost their economy, increase production/job creation, and elevate the quality of life for their people after the mid-20th century communist regimes eroded from 1989–1993 (Amadeo, 2020[b]). The way to do this was simple: become the powerhouse of exports and focus the incoming revenue on infrastructure. China surely

achieved this by having the largest Gross Domestic Product (GDP) by 2010. The US benefitted from China's needs in three ways: "offshoring" labor to reduce the cost to corporations, while decreasing prices in the United States, and furthering the neoliberal globalist economy.

3) From the standpoint of hegemony: having our businesses in China, with so many military bases near China (in Japan, Australia, and South Korea to name a few), allows us to keep "communism in check."

Related to reason number one in the above list is another practical financial reason to keep business in China. At this point, if China liquidates their US Treasury holdings, there would be an economic crisis that would go into critical mass. This is because the United States would be forced to pay their fair share of dividends to the People's Republic of China, and this would bring the international economy that exists now to a grinding halt. Surely, there would be a shift in the paradigm, policies would change, and US businesses may even abandon Beijing and Hong Kong. But the current system is seemingly too cyclical, simple, and profitable for the world of finance to allow such a "tragedy" to come to fruition.

As is true with all systems and cycles, the national debt comes full circle with regard to the China/US relationship, and most economists think the national debt will never actually be paid off (Amadeo, 2020c). So, this is a connected system now of going into debt to pay off debt. To a rationalist, this system is unsustainable and will collapse. To a traditionalist, this system is a financial disaster with no legitimacy. To the everyday US citizen, this is a recipe for doom if the US wants to have a robust domestic labor force which generates its own produce and products. You must be wondering, disregarding the possibility of a full-blown revolution in which the world changes, are there any solutions to this circle of debt and offshoring? The short answer is yes, over time, but the government would have to make foreign and domestic policy changes which are not part of the "new, revised edition of the political playbook." By that I mean, politicians will have to have the guts to alter our current laws regardless of the fact that it may not be popular, or they may not get re-elected. Politicians need to stand for more than re-election, though.

The policy recommendations that most people in the center of the political spectrum would suggest, which the author also suggests, are these:

#1: Reallocate a meager sum of tax money from defense spending to necessary efforts which are listed in the preamble. The preamble has military spending mentioned as well. This section has a lot to offer with regard to government spending: "...Provide for the common defense, promote the general welfare and secure the blessings of liberty to ourselves and our posterity..."; thus, common defense spending could have a small cut to better "promote the general welfare." The author would propose a case management style of helping the homeless, impoverished, and jobless to ensure a prosperous economy (in order to help people and repay the debt faster). The current systems of welfare provided by Health & Human Services could be overhauled with more funding.

#2: Congress or individual states could create a new system of domestic/international business laws. These laws could force companies to at least have an appropriate amount of production in the US. Many companies offshore to avoid paying US citizens their due wages, and they institute headquarters in other countries to avoid taxation. If these practices were halted, there would be an increase in production, GDP, and a decrease in unemployment in the US. As well, the minimum wage needs to be increased. All of this for a better quality of life in the US. (If corporations were given the right to continue their practices but pay hefty fines for the continuation of said practices, they would consider having more production in the US).

#3: Impose taxes on companies which use these legal loopholes to pay little to no taxes. An example is Amazon, which in 2019 paid no income tax to the IRS. Naturally, they generated sales tax but paid none of their own due tax.

#4: Tax raises for the top 10 percent would contribute more money to be used by the government for services to its people.

People may say that it seems unpatriotic to suggest cutting the budget for the Department of Defense (DOD); however, if one takes a purely utilitarian view on the full scope of funding, they would see that it is patriotic to suggest more money be channeled to its citizens. For the fiscal year 2020, the DOD has 721.5 billion dollars at its disposal (defense.gov). Approximately 8 billion dollars of that money must be spent in a mandatory fashion; however, the remaining 713 billion dollars are technically *discretionary*. Over five years, the defense budget is equal to trillions of dollars, and we must ask ourselves, Is that necessary? For example, with appropriate funding, Utah pioneered a program to house the homeless because with case management the homeless population would cost less to house than they do in unpaid emergency room visits, and they are set on a path of success (McKellar, 2019; Scruggs, 2020).

For people on the right of the political spectrum, it must be obvious that the salaries, healthcare, and room and board for all of the soldiers is socialized living for the purposes of defense, which is decried by the right, except when it is a politician or military member who receives those benefits. For people on the left, it must be a "no-brainer" that the US does not need to be the global police force. There are instances where the US should intervene, but the Imperial-Industrial Complex must be analyzed through a practical lens. Is the military trying to instill peace around the globe, or are we modern-day Romans, conquering the known world, "democratizing" nations which are conquered or need help, and punishing those who are not like us with war and trade sanctions?

The author loves the world, and wants world peace, but that is not likely to happen now or by the right hand of the US empire...so, what about the citizens of the US? Why should some of the exorbitant DOD budget not be spent on the people while at the same time limiting deadly conflict and bringing military members home? Should we not stimulate our own economy by channeling willing workers into a robust labor force while simultaneously mandating production to occur in the US? With these changes (and more) would we not be a happier nation, with true patriotic pride, while even paying off some of the national debt?

In the next chapter, we will continue to focus on the side effects of the expansionism and monopolization of corporations from the US. Warfare and its connection to our modern problems of government malfeasance and poor tax allocations, globalizing US businesses, and "ending communism" will come full circle by the end of chapter six. Hopefully, the military and business practices, coupled with the laws of the land, corruption, and abandonment of the middle class, will demonstrate the false narratives of democracy, the reasons for a broken US economy, and global lies that have shaped the fabric of reality for decades. And, hopefully, the solutions that are presented are worthwhile of attention and consideration.

Chapter 5:

The Fourth Industrial Revolution, Monopolies, and the Illusion of Choice

"Where a trust becomes a monopoly, the state has an immediate right to interfere."

~President Theodore Roosevelt

What we have covered so far are the ways in which the Imperial-Industrial Complex extends its reach, laws, and practices to force most of the world to submit to the will of monopolistic companies, conglomerates, and the federal government of the United States. The United States has allowed its companies to dictate the terms of capitalism for so long that it does not even resemble capitalism anymore. This is why the term "oligarchic" was used in a previous chapter, and why a promise that a return to the discussion of Teddy Roosevelt would ensue. An oligarchy is a system of governance in which only a few people control society. Usually a ruling class, the military, and the wealthy elite. In the modern age, an aristocracy of oligarchs would mean that the few who own almost all business and industry work towards a common goal with their government in whichever country where oligarchy reigns supreme. That common goal can mean control over the people, ensuring most profits go to these oligarchs, and/or allowing "business as usual" to encompass social, political, economic, and environmental injustices.

In the age of Teddy Roosevelt's "trust-busting," it was well understood that taking JP Morgan's Northern Securities Company or John D. Rockefeller's Standard Oil to court was a matter of justice. These men were violating the Sherman Antitrust law of 1890, and they were the genesis of how we understand modern monopolies and their creators. The other issue aside from lawbreaking was the crux of capitalism and what it meant to the people of democratic nations. Capitalism is meant to be competitive, and based on the hard work of the citizenry. Capitalism is meant to be a system in which the market relies on this competition to stimulate innovation and maintain fair prices for consumers. When a company can achieve a status of wealth where they buy up all of the opposition, then prices can be fixed, and workers can be paid whatever the monopolist has in mind (in accordance with Department of Labor requirements). And, as has been stated a few times throughout this book, executives can buy political favor in the form of policies which make all of their business practices legal.

In the 21st century, most of the antitrust efforts of the 19th and 20th centuries have been eroded. This quote from *Forbes* magazine displays a concise picture of what we're dealing with regarding monopolies:

> Three companies control about 80% of mobile telecoms. Three have 95% of credit cards. Four have 70% of airline flights within the U.S. Google handles 60% of search...(h/t The Economist) In agriculture, four companies control 66% of U.S. hogs slaughtered in 2015, 85% of the steer, and half the chickens, according to the Department of Agriculture (h/t Open Markets Institute). Similarly, just four companies control 85% of U.S. corn seed sales, up from 60% in 2000, and 75% of soy bean seed, a jump from about half, the Agriculture Department says. Far larger than anyone — the American companies DowDuPont and Monsanto. As we have reported, some economists say this concentration of market power is gumming up the economy and is largely to blame for decades of flat wages and weak productivity growth (Mauldin, 2019).

In recent years, there have been massive mergers and acquisitions that even caught the attention of the Department of Justice (DOJ). AT&T, a company with massive influence, bought Time Warner to keep up with the media titans and maintain its seat of power in the telecommunication industry. The DOJ filed a lawsuit to take AT&T and Time Warner to court, citing classic antitrust issues like competition elimination and too much power. The AT&T merger with Time Warner was approved by the presiding judge, and even an appeal to a higher court by the DOJ was dismissed (CNBC, 2019).

Many mergers seem to occur "without a hitch," such as Disney's meteoric rise to the status of a true monopoly. Disney owns its original content, Star Wars, Marvel, Pixar, National Geographic, ESPN, ABC, Hulu, and a litany of other subsidiaries. In fact, Disney is just one example of five companies that control 90 percent of TV/movies, news channels, and newspapers that US citizens consume on a regular basis. Comcast, Disney, AT&T, Viacom-CBS, and NewsCorp are the aforementioned five companies (Bagdikian, 2004; Littleton, 2018). Food production is dominated by Coca-Cola, Nestle, General Mills, Unilever, Kellogg's, Danone, ABF, Mondelez International (formerly Kraft), and MARS. Finance and insurance are gridlocked by conglomerates like JP Morgan Chase and Berkshire Hathaway. Technology is lorded over by Microsoft and Apple. As mentioned above, and to be further discussed, the trend is irrefutable.

Monopolies are harmful to the economy because of their ability to price- and wage-fix, create dependence on one brand, and they eliminate competition. In the 21st century, US society has seen the death of the brick-and-mortar establishment. The monopolies which control the food and general merchandise trade, like Walmart and Amazon, have sealed this fate of chains and small businesses across the nation. From Sears to Kmart to Blockbuster, hundreds of chain stores have filed for Chapter 11 Bankruptcy, shut down thousands of locations, or completely closed; and then there are the thousands of local stores that you will not find in national newspapers that have also filed for bankruptcy or went out of business (Tyko, 2019).

Aside from being unjust to an international workforce, monopolies are also harmful to their domestic workers. Walmart executives fly in helicopters to fire many employees at one store as soon as there is evidence of a union developing, and Amazon Fulfillment Center employees urinate in bottles to save time while being monitored and criticized at every moment for "low productivity." Wages are at all-time lows in most industries (however, Amazon does have a fifteen-dollar minimum wage), and the percentage of people in private sector unions was 6.2 percent in 2019 (Bureau of Labor Statistics, 2020). "Unionization rates were lowest in farming, fishing, and forestry occupations

(2.1 percent); sales and related occupations (2.8 percent); and food preparation and serving related occupations (3.5 percent)" (Bureau of Labor Statistics, 2020). Despite the outcry for economic justice in the US, the populace is literally buying in on this scheme while Congress does nothing.

Many companies are importing merchandise from China or importing food from Mexico, but the globalization trend is not the only one that allows US companies to either swallow up the competition or eat them alive. Even at the source of US production, this is the status quo. As mentioned in a previous quote, Dow-DuPont and Monsanto are the Agribusiness Colossi (along with Cargill foods) who dominate the production of food, own vast swathes of land in the US, and wholesale to the mercantile companies at rates that traditional farmers cannot compete with in the slightest. And naturally, in the global economy, many items are imported, and some farmers had to resort to exporting. Monopolization and globalization have led to lower prices in the market, but the competition has been eliminated because the "small fish" cannot fight the "big fish" cost-to-price ratio. The "small fish" can be consumed by the "big fish." An alarming and consistent trend is that monopolies buy their opposition or, as noted, run them out of business. This discourtesy is extended to farmers, too, as there has been an increase in farmers simply selling their land and property to the large corporations.

Those in retail can perhaps be more adaptive than the farmers because they can decide that "if you cannot beat them, join them" with regard to transitioning to a retail job that is monopolized. Farmers, however, even if they are paid-off, may have a massive amount of debt to pay, will likely be displaced from their home and land, and have few future job prospects (Semuels, 2019). Consider these quotes from A. Semuels' (2019) article in *Time* magazine entitled "Small American Farmers are Nearing Extinction":

> a trade war, severe weather associated with climate change, tanking commodity prices related to globalization, political polarization, and corporate farming defined not by a silo and a red barn but technology and the efficiencies of scale...is the worst crisis in decades. Chapter 12 farm bankruptcies were up 12 percent in the Midwest from July of 2018 to June of 2019; they're up 50 percent in the Northwest. Tens of thousands have simply stopped farming, knowing that reorganization

> through bankruptcy won't save them. The nation lost more
> than 100,000 farms between 2011 and 2018; 12,000 of those
> between 2017 and 2018 alone...Farm debt, at $416 billion, is
> at an all-time high...Suicides in farm communities are hap-
> pening with alarming frequency.

So, even if a company is in the US, and employs US citizens or visa-holding guest-workers, the quest for business superiority, wealth, and land ownership, compounded with the monopolizing mindset which has been rationalized in corporations, has led to the demise of farmers who are participating in age-old family occupations. The devastating effect of monopolies and globalization on the average blue-collar worker (farmer or factory worker) is two-fold: the jobs vanish to a conglomerate or overseas, and they are not qualified to work in the new positions which require specialized college degrees or vocational training. Technological advancements, specialized careers, and monopolization have all culminated after the globalization of the workforce created the "Rust Belt" in the US. The innovations of monopolies have generated new inventions, medicine, and paradigms of work, but they have never filled the void of the "Rust Belt." Instead, the 21st century has ushered in a new era of the Imperial-Industrial Complex. One which has allowed the United States to be engaged in psychological warfare on itself, finding false enemies everywhere, while exacerbating the foreign operations of this highly technological system which promotes endless consumption and denial of harms.

Robots and "Geniuses" Only: Blue-Collars Need Not Apply

The mechanization of work is as old as work itself. Beyond basic tools like a hammer and chisel, a saw, or a plow hoe, pulleys and cranes, the block-and-tackle, the Archimedes screw, and water mills were all developed by 100 AD. These inventions helped the day laborer, and usually did not render them obsolete. However, in antiquity the masses all had a role in maintaining civilization, the world was not overpopulated, and if one was compelled to change trades, they could take up an apprenticeship and learn a new skill. It is not suggested that becoming a different type of worker would have been easy, but it would have been much easier compared to today's economic atmosphere. In the past one hundred years, when a career has been, or is, mechanized, it usually means massive layoffs, and the people have to scramble to find a new position. On top of that, they have a lot of competition, and they need the req-uisite skills, knowledge, education, or "trainability" that typically white-collar interviewers are looking for. It is even common knowledge that interviewers base your eligibility on how you look, what your name is, and how you behave in one interview.

We are presently living in what has been termed "The Fourth Industrial Revolution." This refers to everything from fully automated factories, which only require a few human workers, to self-scanning at the grocery, to touch-screens, Wi-Fi, smart phones, DNA editing, 3-D printing, biometric scanning, and satellite surveillance and GPS computing. There is a myriad of technol-ogies which have made life easier for some but have completely wiped out job opportunities at the same time. Not only factories, as mentioned above, there has been a revamping of how farming is done: from AI operated watering sys-tems to giant Harvesters which do the work of one week in one day. The in-ventors and engineers for all of these devices must be given their due credit for being so ingenious. Even inventors from Galileo to President Hoover knew that inventions are created to make life easier for humankind; but I do not be-lieve the consequences of hyper-industrialization have been taken into account by multiple parties.

Naturally, the corporations which buy modern technologies for produc-tion or farming knew that they would save money because they would not have to pay wages to a body of employees. In this regard, automation is akin to glob-alization because the companies did a cost-benefit analysis which made robots their low-cost workers in the US as compared to people overseas who work for miniscule amounts of payment. Politicians continue to notice the effects; however, there have been no business laws passed which protect the rights of workers from over-mechanization. One man who has proposed governmental oversight, if not a solution, is Mayor Bill de Blasio of New York City. He has proposed that tax loopholes and subsidies for automation be ended and that a new federal entity be created, entitled the "Federal Automation and Worker Protection Agency," which would mandate severance packages for those losing their jobs to automation. The mayor has also proposed:

> a "robot tax" on large companies that eliminate jobs through
> increased automation and fail to provide adequate replace-
> ment jobs. They'd be required to pay five years of payroll

taxes up front for each employee eliminated. That revenue would go right into a new generation of labor-intensive, high-employment infrastructure projects and new jobs in areas such as health care and green energy that would provide new employment. Displaced workers would be guaranteed new jobs created in these fields at comparable salaries (de Blasio, 2019).

Politicians always "talk a good talk," but they do not "walk a good walk" in the 21st century. That is not to say that Mayor de Blasio's concept is not an intriguing one; it is to say that in the era of our oligarchic republic, we shall never see politicians deviate from deregulation and partisan profitability. In 2008, when President Obama had to take up the reins of a nation in crisis, he favored the side of the banks and business tycoons by bailing them out in his eight-hundred-billion-dollar stimulus bill (Frank, 2017). As previously noted, we are in the era of "too big to fail" and "too small to succeed". President Obama's stimulus bill did contain many noble efforts: "subsidies for clean-energy projects, a push to update medical record-keeping, billions for high-speed rail projects and support for a long list of state and local construction schemes" (Frank, 2017).

However, the stimulus bill did not create jobs through federal programs, and it legitimized the criminal behavior of those in banking and investment. Banks, stockbrokers, and businessmen regularly create predatory lending and pyramid schemes, invest in business which is deemed illegal by the international community, and create shell corporations in "tax havens" which offer no services to the public and launder money which has been obtained via insider trading, illegal investment strategies, or siphoning money from phony accounts. Yet, even though white-collar crime costs the US billions of dollars every year, "Federal prosecutions for white-collar crimes hit a twenty-year low in 2015" (Frank, 2017). And please, do not take this critique of President Obama to mean that it is one person's fault that the cycle repeats itself. There are systems in place to control people, politicians namely, and it is because they metaphorically "sleep with the enemy" instead of using their authority to combat corrupt business practices. President Obama is not the first president to be scorned in this book, and he will not be the last; but the scorning must be finished to move on.

With regard to ending the cycle of "trickle-down" hypocrisy, and creating work for the impoverished and lower middle-class alike, the Obama Administration engaged in inaction. The former president had decried NAFTA as a campaigner but then supported it and the Walmart- and Silicon Valley-backed Trans-Pacific Partnership once president. He had been appalled at the wealth of the top 10 percent who profit from banking and business deregulation, until his inauguration and then the stimulus bailout. And he, like so many other democrats, was a member of the "Party of the People" until he was a member of the "Party of the Billionaire and Ivory Tower" (Frank, 2017).

One admirable attempt of the Obama-era was the creation of environmental standards, which would create new jobs and eventually transition workers from perhaps a coal mine to a solar plant. Most of these plans are being deregulated. Naturally, the greatest thing which came out of the Obama Administration for the people of the United States was the Affordable Care Act, the landmark healthcare bill. But that was a Band-Aid on the amputation inflicted on the body of the American workforce over the past forty years.

The state-corporate relationship has always been seen as a typical Modus Operandi for the Republican Party, but sometime at the end of the 20th century, the Democrats converted. Namely, the Clinton Administration. The Bush, Obama, and Trump administrations have been simple continuations of the "Revolving Door" of academics and businessmen becoming government professionals and creating policies which legitimize the oppressive corporate practices seen in our country and abroad. In the Clinton, Bush, Obama, and Trump administrations, millions of dollars were contributed to their party at large, which helps guarantee reelections and ensures preferential treatment toward those making donations. This mutual support system upholds current foreign and domestic state-corporate structures.

Obama's 2011 State of the Union speech indicated his full one-hundred-and-eighty-degree turn by saying "So yes, the world has changed. The competition for jobs is real" (Frank, 2017). There was no hope in his words; the American people simply needed to blindly accept the "inevitable" tide of the Fourth Industrial Revolution. However, this tide is only inevitable if government continues to revolve around business. Unfortunately, as has been mentioned in this text, the cyclical pattern of business supporting political parties or members (via direct donations, lobbyists, SuperPACs, or Non-Profits), and then the government giving them the policies, deregulation, tax cuts, or subsidies they require, is a vexing reality that has even been upheld by the Supreme Court of the United States. The case I am referring to is *Citizens United v. FEC*.

Citizens United versus the Federal Election Commission

In the 2008 election, the US saw the typical, incessant onslaught of smear campaigns on television. The smear campaigns are directed at either the Democrats or Republicans, and they are often full of *ad hominem* attacks. Usually they will indicate that someone campaigning wants to "take away your guns," "ruin our healthcare system," "cripple us with taxes," "help billionaires, not working people," "destroy education in the US," or "privatize everything, eliminating services which should be government-run." Citizens United is one of many 501(c) non-profit groups which produce advertisements like these, and in 2008 their attack was against Hillary Clinton. Organizations who produce these campaign advertisements, and most activities of organizations which support political candidates, used to have limits on how much they could spend per election cycle. The Federal Election Commission (FEC) halted the airing of the Citizens United advertisement against Hillary Clinton due to spending limits, and Citizens United took the issue to the Supreme Court. After *Citizens United v. FEC*, there were no spending limits for independent groups who supported or criticized candidates in the media, as long as they were not "coordinating" with a campaign.

As Lau (2019) put it:

> With its decision, the Supreme Court overturned election spending restrictions that date back more than 100 years. Previously, the court had upheld certain spending restrictions, arguing that the government had a role in preventing corruption. But in *Citizens United*, a bare majority of the justices held that "independent political spending" did not present a substantive threat of corruption, provided it was not coordinated with a candidate's campaign. As a result, corporations can now spend unlimited funds on campaign advertising if they are not formally "coordinating" with a candidate or political party.

Now, a big source of confusion in the US revolves around campaign finance laws. Here's a rundown of what a business or individual can give: $2,800 to federal candidates per election, up to $5,600 a year; $5,000 per year to traditional Political Action Committees (PACs—they are not the same as Super-PACs); $10,000 per year to State or Local Party Federal accounts; $35,500 per year to the main account of National Party Committees; $106, $500 per year to the RNC or DNC convention accounts; $106, 500 per year to the party building accounts of National Party Committees; $106,500 per year to the legal fund of the National Party Committees (Longley, 2019). As mentioned above, SuperPACs are not traditional PACs, and ever since *Citizens United*, they have been able to take unlimited donations and spend unlimited amounts to support candidates in the media as long as they are not formally "coordinating" with the campaign in question. SuperPACs have to disclose their donors, but the non-profits which give them funds do not. The non-profit and SuperPAC loophole of undisclosed donors is often termed "dark money."

So, yes, the political economy is as obnoxiously complicated as you would expect. What all of this means is that the companies are able to channel their money through groups who support candidates on television, or smear those they do not like, and with traditional campaign finance, they can pay for a candidate's entire campaign (travel, food, staffing, extra expenditures, etc.). Unless someone is taking out cash via embezzlement or money laundering, it is not common for politicians in the US to receive money directly from corporations. Traditionally, politicians release their tax returns and disclose "gifts" they may have claimed. Those gifts are usually an inheritance or something of that nature. However, they could get a gift, and they only have to disclose it in the obscure range of five million to twenty-five million dollars. Money given to someone else to give to a politician as a gift, or money put into another bank account for a politician, is a possibility; however, this is a gray area, and any observations on that kind of illegal money are pure speculation.

Instead, what corporations have paid for is influence and power. They have paid for an entire campaign and have supported candidates with a television presence that they may not have been able to afford. Once the preferred candidate is in place, it is easy for a company's executives to be in constant communication with the politician of choice. The politician recognizes that they have been given their seat of authority with a massive amount of help from the corporations in question, and they are very susceptible to the will of monopolies. The reason they are so susceptible is because they want to be ree-lected, and without the resources of the supporting companies, they will not succeed. As well, corporations can easily blackmail the politicians by telling them they will support another candidate in the next election cycle and smear them all at the same time.

This is one area where the "power of the people" comes into play. The CEOs of monopolies know all too well that advertisements are a powerful tool for swaying people's votes. They know this from political research as well as market research. Manipulation of the populace through the media is some-thing that monopolies have an expertise in. An array of subconscious ideas has been planted into people's minds: you must go into debt to experience the "American Dream"; you need to eat out four times a week; you must put a dia-mond worth two months' salary on your fiancé's finger; if you are not buying something new or staying "fit," then you are not living your best life. The list could surely go on and on. This phenomenon has become so common, and the information is worth so much money, it is why we have seen Google, Ama-zon, Facebook, and other online companies start to sell your search histories. Companies pay a pretty penny to know what you want to buy, and how you want to vote, and they pay for premiere advertisement placement on your Google and Facebook via algorithms. In reality, Google and Facebook make most of their money off of advertisements. And advertisements have always been a large portion of company expenditures—because they work.

How much money has been spent by SuperPACs since *Citizens United*? It has been reported that $2.9 billion has been spent on federal elections since the Supreme Court decision, and the top one hundred donors contributed ap-proximately 78 percent of those funds (Lau, 2019; Massoglia, 2020). For ex-ample, the Center for Responsive Politics and the *Washington Post* did an investigation into the 2012 election cycle. They found that seventeen groups raised $407 million from the billionaire Koch brothers, which mostly went into advertising against President Obama (Editorial Board, 2014). On the other side of the coin, liberal groups spent more money through Super PACs than their conservative counterparts for the first time in 2018. Two non-profits of note, "Majority Forward" and "Sixteen Thirty Fund," have given millions of dollars to Democrat-associated Super PACs (Massoglia, 2020). And, as said before, these non-profits are not disclosing their donors to the government, which makes the investigation much more difficult. As seen above, the Center for Responsive Politics had to track the corporations which donated to non-profits via tax returns. The non-profit then gives to the Super PACs. Without watchdogs, the populace would not be made aware of these identities; and sometimes they are still a mystery.

The Illusion of Choice

What has been illustrated through this chapter are the tentacles of monopolies: how they offshore work while simultaneously destroying competition in their homeland, how they use their exorbitant wealth to influence the masses and politics, and how they have converted democratic capitalism into oligarchy. Monopolies have utilized wealth to perform this alchemy of political economy, which allows them to profit as much as possible. The illusion of choice is the concept that people feel as if they have an abundance of options in their sphere of existence, but in reality, they are only choosing what has carefully been presented to them. In other words, the choices have been made for you, and even though you have some options, you are only choosing between which monopolies to support.

The conglomerates and monopolies inculcate a slew of messages and indoctrinated thought through media and business practices, and at the end of each "choice" you make, you have supported their cause through a vote or patronage. When you buy food, you are only choosing between a few producers and suppliers. When you read the news or watch television, you are consuming stories that have been selected by a handful of executives in five or six companies. When you pump your gasoline, you have unwittingly selected between a few oil conglomerates. When you choose most of your technology services, the choices are even fewer. When you choose a career in the private sector, you are usually choosing between conglomerates and monopolies who will overwork and underpay you based on inflation and historic rates. When you work in the public sectors of government, you will be working for beneficiaries of the illusion of choice. Because, lastly, when you vote for a politician, you are generally choosing between the politicians which have been selected by the elite of business and finance to become representatives.

As was stated earlier in this book, you will vote for a representative, but they will act on everything that matters. International and domestic business laws, war, safety and transparency regulations, wage standards, insurance policies, and anti-corruption measures will all be discussed in the House of Representative or the Senate. Before anything is ever produced on Capitol Hill, the two-party system can remain at a standstill because they only vote based on what their party dictates. And the party, generally, only votes on what their donors desire. However, a Bill can be introduced, and can easily be dismissed without enough votes. The House can pass a Bill, and the Senate can reject it. A Bill could be presented to the president, and he can veto it. The president can create an Executive Order, and it can be blocked by a federal judge; or he can pick people for his Cabinet and a starstruck, lobbied-out Senate will say "Yes, sir" to whomever is chosen. So, with the Checks and Balance System embroiled in an oligarchy and childish bids for reelection, even the government is prey to the illusion of choice. They either choose ideological compromise or inaction. And, once again, "we the people" have no say.

The past four years have demonstrated that the "Revolving Door" does not stop rotating. President Trump stated that he would "drain the swamp," supposedly indicating that lobbyist influence would be limited and former business executives would no longer hold high offices in government. Absolutely none of that has occurred. President Trump hired Steve Mnuchin and James Donovan as Treasury Secretary and Deputy Treasury Secretary, respectively, and both are former Goldman Sachs executives (Firozi, 2017). Gary Cohn, head of the National Economic Council, was a Goldman Sachs employee, and Steve Bannon, the former chief strategist for the current Cabinet, was also a Sachs man. After James Mattis was Secretary of Defense, President Trump selected Patrick Shanahan, a former Boeing executive, to be the leader of the Pentagon (Macias, 2019). The current Environmental Protection Agency (EPA) administrator, Andrew Wheeler, is a former fossil fuel lobbyist who is working to eliminate a Clean Power Plan "and replace it with a proposed rule to set state guidelines for power-plant emissions of greenhouse gases that contribute to a warming planet." And his agency finalized revisions to a 2015 Obama-era rule regulating the disposal of coal ash that gives states and utilities what he called "'much needed flexibility' to manage their waste" (King, 2019). The list goes on and on.

President Trump's time in office has also displayed some of the threats posed by foreign governments. Of particular interest to this discussion is that the *Citizens United* decision has allowed foreign donations to go undetected. Since the non-profits who fund Super PACs do not have to disclose their donors, there is much suspicion that foreign governments and businesses have had a vested interest in US elections since 2010 (Lau, 2019; Massoglia, 2020). This is a violation of long-standing election laws. And since Russian operatives and internet "bots" were involved in manipulating voters with fraudulent advertisements and statements in 2016, along with the usual influx of political commercials, it has been clear to see the influence that foreign governments wish to have in the US—either for economic or military favors.

President Trump's farce of an impeachment trial began because he was leveraging military aid to Ukraine for information on Joe Biden and his son. Ukraine has been in conflict with Russia since the dissolution of the USSR. It seems as if President Trump was irresolute in sending military aid to that country particularly because he is indifferent if Russia conquers them. People can easily be influenced to be indifferent, especially if their campaign is funded by foreign governments. As well, President Trump is more voracious in his transparency about one thing that other politicians will deny: his need to be feared, loved, and reelected. However, as stated before, the current president is not the first nor last to work with despots—but usually the US does not side with Russia for historic reasons mentioned earlier. China and Iran have equal motive and opportunity to fund the liberal side (Becket and Gazis, 2020).

One of the most unfortunate societal side effects of the illusion of choice in the US has been misguided hate. For example, we are a nation with a wealth of exceptional diversity, and that includes our mixed political economy. You may think you fully support capitalism, and despise socialism, but both are in our country. Social security, welfare, unemployment, and the Affordable Care Act are socialist notions playing out in our society. They are generally misunderstood, mismanaged, and/or underfunded to the point of ineffective. However, they are a security net that is needed for the populace, and which should be governed more competently. Some people claim to hate capitalism, but capitalism allows for a flourishing market of commerce and ideas. Instead, what they hate is economic inequality, which stems from lax regulation of capitalism. Both ideologies would claim to hate certain politicians, which creates sociopolitical division and anger in the streets, but in reality, what they all should hate is a common enemy. A system which has allowed businesses to determine which politicians are candidates, and the influence over them to continue the inequalities that affect every working US citizen and many more. Republicans and Democrats have both contributed to this system.

For the masses, a consolidated unity on these matters would create a galvanized protest base to petition grievances of lobbyism, offshoring, fair pay, affordable medical coverage, and many other issues. As well, a more humane attitude could permeate our civil and political discourse which understands the simple fact that almost all people are struggling with this systematized "Fugazi" of democracy. When it comes to polarization in this country, what has been noticeable in the past five to ten years is that people dismiss others' beliefs and criticize them with such animosity that, naturally, groups were formed. These groups operate on the premise that everything the other group says is wrong, which shows a clear lack of sympathy and willingness to reason on the basis of humanity. The tribal and clique aspects of these groups are appealing to the human nature to conform and to feel accepted. Furthermore, when there is a movement, there will always be a countermovement; there is no doubt about that. However, the arts of negotiation and compromise have been lost on the past two generations. Their illusion is that they have to choose between one group or the other, or one party or the other, when, truly, there is a middle-ground available that appeals to logic and the rule of law.

Here is the part of the chapter where policy recommendations are offered up which could be to the benefit, and reconciliation, of those who have been polarized by the problems of the 21st century. The needs and rationale of those affected are not the same, but if appropriate laws were made, then an overarching amelioration of inequities could be addressed. The following policy recommendations will be aimed at monopolies, workers' rights, campaign finance, and lobbyism. They are by no means the only policies which could be enacted.

#1: Enforce Antitrust Laws from the top down to eliminate monopolies. Dissolve particularly malignant monopolies.

#2: As has been mentioned in previous chapters, force more production to happen in the US.

#3: Require disclosure from non-profit donors in political campaigns. And start a legal lockdown on lobbyism practices.

#4: Continue creating work opportunities in energy and mainland production; direct companies to make side-by-side working in automated industries a reality.

#5: And, along with all other policy recommendations made in this book, raise the minimum wage. Because until there is an overhaul of work in the US, monopolies need to pay people adequately. They may get away with it overseas, and they should not, but they must not be allowed to offer such a disservice to their homeland.

Chapter 6:

Modern Warfare, the USA Freedom Act, and the Military-Industrial Complex

"The national security establishment ... this bureaucracy and class of special emergency managers ... are able to control policy on a national scale because they perpetrate and then benefit from a continuing state of emergencies. Their power is contingent on extraordinary security circumstances, and those circumstances never end ... They have become self-sustaining, a shadow legal system, one that I wrote was commensurate to a bloodless coup. A perpetual state of emergency, of threat, and of panic is the necessary precondition for this American coup to persist. We have that in perpetual war and in the constant specter that we are fed ... that some thin line of their security efforts barely separates us from another 9/11. But we also have it now ... in addition ... in the threat of cyber everything ... from election hacking to our own personal identity theft ... Or substitute climate change ... Any ubiquitous threat with no actual solution, one that affects everyone's life, but one that also has an apocalyptic element to it ... it is how we describe a world that is so terrifying and out of our control that we ultimately need to turn it over to technocrats."

~William Arkin in his speech: How the News Media, and the Public, Contribute to Perpetual War

War has changed. War used to be fought on the ground, and it was fought with weapons that made battles visceral—not clinical. The army with the greatest numbers did not always win, but regardless of numbers, the goal was almost never total annihilation. The goal of Empire was to conquer the known world, subjugate it, tax it, and then assimilate it into the world of the victor. The majority of wars throughout all time have been links in a singular chain which is characterized by the hubris of kings, the ethnocentrism of a nation, and the need to conquer neighbors and enemies alike because they are "inferior."

From the Hittites to the Persians, to the Greeks and Romans, they all saw a vision of an Earth that was ruled by one Empire. This pattern did not die out as civilizations marched forward into the timeline of Anno Domini; in reality it intensified. The Holy Roman Empire reassembled the last vestiges of the Roman Empire, and many branches of the papal power nexus had their turn at being the leader of Europe. The seat of the Holy Roman Empire was in Germany, and had been since Charlemagne was crowned Holy Roman Emperor in 800 AD. Although the Prussian King Frederick the Great, in the 1700s, was still technically a Holy Roman Emperor, the Germans and Italians were always too divided into jurisdictions to be a true Empire. The Spanish went to the New World, but even they would be outshined by the next Empire to surpass their impressive expansion: the British Empire. As has been noted on many occasions: "the sun never set on the British Empire."

The British paid for and took many slaves, and they fought several wars from the Revolutionary War in America to the Opium Wars in China. However, the sentiment still existed with the British that civilians should be left out of warfare unless unavoidable. The sentiment ranged from ancient to near-modern wars that arrangements should be made to avoid killing non-combatants. After all, the point of expansion was to put the newly subjugated into your sphere of influence as partners and extensions of your Empire. With too many dead, too much hostility and lack of a citizenry would make the conquering less industrious.

Civilians were often left out of wars, although their regimes and culture may have hung in the balance. As well, women would have been spoils of war in many ages, meaning that many were raped and/or taken as wives. And some of the civilians would have been made slaves. There have been many exceptions to avoiding non-combatants even in antiquity, such as the ancient genocide at Carthage, medieval attempts to destroy all Saracens in the Crusades, the Mongolian invasion of China, and the 30 Years War in mainland Europe. Each one of those examples had a devastating effect on the populace, and much of the difference will be seen in the differences in the purpose of the war in question. If certain wars are for Empire, then there should not be eradication; that would be reserved for a hated enemy which needs wiped off of the face of the planet. If other wars are against a particular tyranny, then they are based on fighting to reduce morale and show no mercy. By the 20th century, despite differences in kind, we see all former attempts to omit civilian casualties removed from the moral compass.

There have been claims that 80–90 percent of modern-era war victims have been citizens, not combatants; however, that statistic has been disputed due to its vague terminologies and lack of empirical evidence (Roberts, 2010). But what is understood, by academics, human rights organizations, five-star generals, and those stricken by war, is that civilians do pay a heavy toll in modern war. The ratio may not be nine to one, meaning that 90 percent of people killed are civilians versus 10 percent being soldiers, but the death rate of citizens is high despite the official numbers being difficult to calculate. The numbers are equivocal because famine, disease, suicides, and displacement have been utilized in projections and reports, and other times, it is because so many have been buried that accurate numbers are difficult to approximate.

The World Wars changed the nature of combat, from trench warfare, to tanks, to white phosphorous usage, automatic weapons, planes, bombs, and, eventually, the hydrogen bomb. In Vietnam, Agent Orange was used. As will be discussed below, various chemical and biological agents have been used around the globe in warfare. But now, we have moved into the era of the drone. We have also moved into the era of the "War on Terror." This "War on Terror" has been heralded as peace in the Middle East by the Pentagon, and has been decried as an abject failure, with amorphous enemies and ulterior motives, by researchers, journalists, and human rights organizations.

What will be beneficial to the investigation at hand is another case study, and one that wholly focuses on 9/11 and the "War on Terror." The information will lend insight into the various ways in which the Imperial-Industrial Complex has maneuvered during this complex period which has lasted since 2001. The ways in which the military continues its trend of "democratization" and occupation while businesses establish themselves in licit or illicit fashions for access to the resources available during a time of chaos will be a central focus of the case study. As well, the civilian death toll will be summoned to display some of the unnecessary carnage that can take place in a modern war.

The differences in technology and warfare will be useful in understanding the Empire game at its most sophisticated.

After this case study, a transition to how the "War on Terror" affects US citizens' civil liberties will occur, because once something begins with the military, it can trickle to citizens. This has been noteworthy in political and technological matters. The Cold War and the civil rights movement displayed the paranoid and power-hungry nature of the FBI and CIA, as they killed political activists and civil rights leaders, and as they spied on anyone who seemed like a threat to the status quo of infallibility of government. In our modern age, almost every piece of digital technology was used by the military before it was used by civilians: computers, GPS, cell phones, and much more. Ironically, those same handy devices are now able to be used for spying and tracking in a way the FBI and CIA wish they could have had back in the 1960s.

A Case Study of the Iraq War: Its History and its Future Implications

On the morning of Tuesday, September 11th, 2001, at 8:45 a.m., a Boeing 767 plane loaded with enough fuel to travel to California crashed into the north tower of the World Trade Center. Then, eighteen minutes later, the south tower was struck by another Boeing 767 while the north tower was attempting an evacuation (History, 2018). Meanwhile, the Pentagon had another plane on a collision course impact it, while yet another landed in a field in Pennsylvania. Nearly three thousand people died from the terrorist attacks of 9/11, most of them in New York City (History, 2010). One hundred eighty-nine people died in the destruction at the Pentagon, including the people on the plane. Forty-four people died in the plane that crashed in Pennsylvania, and it only crashed where it did due to a rebellion of the passengers once they heard about the other attacks. It has been called the darkest day in American history.

The terrorists were nineteen men of various Arabic descent, most of them from Saudi Arabia. The al-Qaeda, a militant group governed by Saudi fugitive Osama bin Laden, reportedly funded the attacks (History, 2018). The reasons for the attacks were political and ideological. Al-Qaeda wanted to retaliate against the US for the Persian Gulf War, and for the US's continued military presence in the Middle East coupled with its support for Israel (History, 2018). The reason for the Iraq War is more oblique than the destructive counterbalance al-Qaeda wished to exact. As stated above, almost everyone involved in the hijacking of the planes, and the leader of the commissioning party, were from Saudi Arabia. And it must be mentioned that the US was already at war with the Taliban in Afghanistan. Al-Qaeda and the Taliban are distinct in nationality and function and, naturally, are not from Iraq. A point which will be returned to shortly.

The US declared war on Iraq on March 19th, 2003, and by March 22nd, the world was able to watch the televised bombing of Baghdad. Mosul, Kirkuk, Basra, and Nasiriyah were all bombed that night, from strategic positions of battleships in the Red Sea and Persian Gulf, and from the F-14 Tomcats and F/A-18 Hornet strike planes in the air. This night raid of blitzkrieg, and veritable seismic event, was dubbed "Shock and Awe." The technique has been in the military playbook for quite some time, and the US had an excellent target for occupation and democratization.

As mentioned in chapter three, the CIA supported installing Saddam Hussein as the leader of Iraq in 1959. In 1958 a communist supporter, General Abd al-Karim Qasim, had committed a regicide by killing the Iraqi monarchs in a bloody coup d'état (Sale, 2003). To conform to the anti-communism pattern of the US military and CIA eliminating supporters of communism, they allied themselves with Saddam Hussein to assassinate the new Prime Minister Qasim. Many former CIA and Military officials provided accounts to Robert Sale for his 2003 investigative report "Saddam Key in Early CIA Plot." Sale (2003) describes the CIA relationship with Saddam toppling Qasim like this:

> Adel Darwish, Middle East expert and author of "Unholy Babylon," said the move was done "with full knowledge of the CIA," and that Saddam's CIA handler was an Iraqi dentist working for CIA and Egyptian intelligence. U.S. officials separately confirmed Darwish's account. Darwish said that Saddam's paymaster was Capt. Abdel Maquid Farid, the assistant military attaché at the Egyptian Embassy who paid for the apartment from his own personal account. Three former senior U.S. officials have confirmed that this is accurate. The assassination was set for Oct. 7, 1959, but it was completely botched. Accounts differ. One former CIA official said that the 22-year-old Saddam lost his nerve and began firing too soon, killing Qasim's driver and only wounding Qasim in the

shoulder and arm. Darwish told UPI that one of the assassins had bullets that did not fit his gun and that another had a hand grenade that got stuck in the lining of his coat. "It bordered on farce," a former senior U.S. intelligence official said. But Qasim, hiding on the floor of his car, escaped death, and Saddam, whose calf had been grazed by a fellow would-be assassin, escaped to Tikrit, thanks to CIA and Egyptian intelligence agents, several U.S. government officials said. Saddam then crossed into Syria and was transferred by Egyptian intelligence agents to Beirut, according to Darwish and former senior CIA officials. While Saddam was in Beirut, the CIA paid for Saddam's apartment and put him through a brief training course, former CIA officials said. The agency then helped him get to Cairo, they said.

Eventually, with prior approval from JFK, Saddam's Ba'ash Party gained power by killing their enemies, the Qasim regime, in 1963. By the 1970s, the strained relationship between Iran and Iraq was palpable. Subsequently, the Iran-Iraq War began in September of 1980, and the Reagan Administration wanted to ensure that Iraq did not lose. There were many reasons, but the most important were that 1) Iran could infiltrate US oil supplies in Kuwait and Iraq if they gained a foothold, 2) Saddam Hussein had been a friend of the US government in the past and perhaps he could continue the anti-communist trend with this war, and 3) Iran could destabilize Middle East allies such as Saudi Arabia, Israel, and Jordan (Dobbs, 2002). Iraq was removed from the State Department terrorism list in 1982, and the Reagan Administration began covert anti-communism efforts on a large scale (Dobbs, 2002).

Iraq was only able to overcome their Iranian foes with the assistance of the US, Germany, and Britain—the assistance ranged from satellite information, military intelligence, weapons, and even chemical and biological agents. As Dobbs (2002) detailed:

A review of thousands of declassified government documents and interviews with former policymakers shows that U.S. intelligence and logistical support played a crucial role in shoring up Iraqi defenses against the "human wave" attacks by suicidal Iranian troops. The administrations of Ronald Reagan and George H.W. Bush authorized the sale to Iraq of numerous items that had both military and civilian applications, including poisonous chemicals and deadly biological viruses, such as anthrax and bubonic plague.

The usage of those weapons was a clear violation of the Geneva Conventions, but this was all allowable for realpolitik. Realpolitik is a favorite rationalization of the US government, meaning that anything is allowable, and by all means necessary, if it furthers the larger agenda of the US government (or business) as a whole, not just as a military or democracy. As stated previously, the US has ratified the Geneva Conventions but has not ratified the Rome Statute of the International Criminal Court (ICC). This means that a US head of state could not be prosecuted by the ICC for providing those weapons, and that similar powerful professionals could not be tried for war crimes or crimes of aggression. Before 2002, there was no ICC. Naturally, Saddam Hussein was hanged after prosecution for his actions in Kuwait. The US could take its own people to court for violating the Geneva Conventions, but we all know that is just not going to happen. But back to the story.

One thing that must be noted about the Iran-Iraq War is the timeline: it lasted from 1980 until 1988. During this time, even though the US was staunchly supporting Iraq, the Reagan Administration took its anti-communism efforts to massively hypocritical and ironic proportions. The Reagan Administration facilitated the 1986 Iran-Contra affair, in which Iran bought missiles and other arms from the US, violating a US trade embargo against Iran, and Iran secured the release of seven American hostages in Lebanon; the money received for the weapons was utilized to assist a Nicaraguan coup which would result in an allied government south of the equator (History, 2017). So, in that twist of events, the US was giving weapons to Iran and Iraq during a highly destructive period in which inconsistency would have been unthinkable. Yet, it happened; and that is not the first, nor last, time the US has supported both sides of a conflict. To the military-industrial complex, and as realpolitik, it is simple supply and demand.

Hussein became our enemy by 1990 when he invaded Kuwait, and then the proceeding Gulf War ensued. Congress created, and Bill Clinton signed into law, the "Iraq Liberation Act," and Congress created the Rumsfeld

Commission to investigate intelligence matters in the Defense sector and the CIA (Heilbrunn, 2020). The Commission was named after Donald Rumsfeld, the envoy to Iraq in the 1980s who brokered so many unofficial diplomatic agreements between Iraq and the US—having met with Saddam Hussein many times and assuring him that the US and Iraq were allies (Dobbs, 2002; Heilbrunn, 2020; Morphonios, 2014). Rumsfeld was a three-term Congressman from Illinois in the 1960s, was made a Representative to NATO, and was the Secretary of Defense from 1975–77 under Gerald Ford. Rumsfeld was also appointed as the Secretary of Defense for a second time, serving from 2001–2006 under President George W. Bush.

The CIA was criticized by Rumsfeld and others for its lack of transparency about the "threat level" of Saddam Hussein during the proceedings of the Rumsfeld Commission. Hussein became a power-hungry man on his own; however, many accounts show he was isolated and ousted people from his inner circle instead of inviting terrorists into his reign (Dobbs, 2002; Sale, 2003). But after 9/11, then Vice President Dick Cheney, a protégé of Donald Rumsfeld, imposed immense pressure on the former CIA director George Tenet to claim that Saddam Hussein had ties to al-Qaeda and possessed weapons of mass destruction. For a fact, no weapons of mass destruction were ever found in Iraq, and most reporters, like Bob Woodward and Robert Draper, have concluded that the CIA never had a solid case that Iraq was connected to al-Qaeda (Heilbrunn, 2020; History, 2018). But details of that nature were not important to those who were attempting to quell a nation's panic with another war, spread the idea that peace comes from war, and, mainly, profit from war. National Security Council meetings about apportioning the land to the US and allies, and a Halliburton letter to the Pentagon about oil-infrastructure, were all hatched for many months before the 9/11 attack (Hiro, 2007).

The Iraq War cost the US taxpayers $1.7 trillion, and every bit of that money spent was spent on a lie to the American public (Young, 2013). Fifteen of the nineteen hijackers during the 9/11 attacks were from Saudi Arabia, two were from the United Arab Emirates, and one was from Egypt (CNN, 2020). That is not to say that their countries explicitly supported them, most were in fact exiled or renegades, but it is to say that none of them were from Iraq. Furthermore, there has never been any proof that Saddam Hussein had any relationship with al-Qaeda. In reality, the US placed him in his seat of power, and for that, he would most likely have been forever grateful.

Iraq had nothing to do with 9/11; however, they were a convenient scapegoat because the CIA needed to have their messy dictator eradicated, and the US needed to protect its oil fields. On top of that, the Iraq War was fraught with corruption from private contractors and human rights abuses against citizens. Vice President Dick Cheney, who, upon returning to government service, installed his daughter as the CEO of his Texas-based oil company Halliburton, urged intervention because he knew of the profits to be reaped. Halliburton's subsidiary company, Kellogg, Brown & Root (KBR), an engineering and construction company "was given $39.5 billion in Iraq-related contracts over the past decade, with many of the deals given without any bidding from competing firms, such as a $568-million contract renewal in 2010 to provide housing, meals, water and bathroom services to soldiers, a deal that led to a Justice Department lawsuit over alleged kickbacks..." (Young, 2013).

As well, around one hundred thousand to three hundred thousand barrels (or between five to fifteen million dollars) of Iraqi oil production were missing daily according to the Government Accountability Office (Hendren, 2007). It is notable that Iraq was under a UN oil embargo since the invasion of Kuwait, but that Halliburton and many other companies had purchased smuggled oil from Iraq during that period (Hendren, 2007; Tyagi, 2019). A speculation could be that much of the oil that went missing during the years of the war went to companies like Halliburton and other private interests from around the globe. Iraq has the second largest oil reserves in the world, behind Saudi Arabia, and this was a chance to privatize what was originally government-subsidized for the benefit of the Iraqi populace. All of these quotes truly sum up the main consensus of the purpose of the Iraq War:

> "Of course it's about oil; we can't really deny that," said Gen. John Abizaid, former head of U.S. Central Command and Military Operations in Iraq, in 2007. Former Federal Reserve Chairman Alan Greenspan agreed, writing in his memoir, "I am saddened that it is politically inconvenient to acknowledge what everyone knows: the Iraq war is largely about oil." Then-Sen. and now Defense Secretary Chuck Hagel said the same in 2007: "People say we're not fighting for oil. Of course we are" (Juhasz, 2013).

President George W. Bush was swindled during all of this too. The president, who was new to the game and believed in noble ideas about spreading democracy around the world, was most likely not aware of the entire backstory of the US-Iraq relationship, nor the obvious ulterior motives presented by his Cabinet. President Bush fired Rumsfeld and pushed Cheney to the side by 2006, presumably after he learned of Iraq's lack of connection to al-Qaeda, and the corruption and lying of his Administration (Heilbrunn, 2020). However, by that time, the Iraq War was in full effect and pulling out all of the troops would have left Iraq in a gridlock of private companies and a crippled infrastructure with no military presence to attempt to keep the peace. The Iraq War is what created mass chaos in Iraq, and there is no doubt about that.

Regarding the actual military circumstances of the Iraq War, the army released its Iraq War Study in 2018. The study concluded that Iran was the only winner of this long and grueling conflict (South, 2019). There were not enough soldiers to launch a full-scale occupation, which is why it was rife for private contractors' malfeasance, and there is the reality that the war could have been avoided entirely. President Bush, according to Robert Draper and Bob Woodward, did not want to go to war until he was given phony information by Cheney and Rumsfeld. According to the Department of Defense, there were 4,431 US soldier deaths in Iraq from 2003–2011 (defense.gov). The civilian body count ranges from 185,296–208,295 casualties (iraqbodycount.org). Osama bin Laden, the leader of al-Qaeda, was killed in 2011 in his hideout in Pakistan (not Iraq), and the technical end of the war was also in 2011.

As has been noted, the war ended, but the democratic restructuring efforts, privatization of oil, and private security for the US embassy in Iraq all continued well into 2016–17. Ostensibly, the US Navy SEALs could have assassinated Osama bin Laden without an entire war; covert operations happen all over the globe. Also, with diplomacy and tact, most combatant and non-combatant casualties could have been avoided. What also could have been prevented is the chaos of ISIS and the social disintegration in Iraq. Many experts have stated that ISIS manifested because of the conditions of the Iraq War; because nothing radicalizes young men like a war-torn country with consistent bombings, death, and military occupation. ISIS may have called themselves "al-Qaeda in Iraq" (AQI) at first, but the connection developed long after 9/11 and was an effect of the Iraq War rather than a cause.

So, speaking of another problem that the US National Security Establishment created and aimed to fix, we can delve into the topic of the Islamic State of Iraq and al-Sham (ISIS). The author of the quote at the beginning of this chapter, William Arkin, was a longstanding contributor to NBC and other media outlets, and he is a military expert, researcher, and author. As he said in the quote, and on numerous other occasions, national security officials perpetrate and then benefit from a continuing state of emergencies. This has become more evident with the "War on Terror" than in any other era in US military history. This war is an ongoing conflict with no end in sight, mainly because it provides trillions of dollars to defense every few years. This is not to say that ISIS are not violent people who have wreaked havoc on their own, but it is to say that they did not exist until a shellshocked adolescent group grew up in the Iraq War and needed an outlet for their rage. As Arkin and others have pointed out, the US inadvertently created ISIS, and this has given credence to the amorphous "War on Terror."

In recent years, the United States' Department of Defense (DOD) budget is regularly over $700 billion a year, and was increasing from 2010 to 2019. The DOD budget was $738 billion in 2019, and had a decrease to $721.5 billion in 2020 due to budget cuts for stimulus checks related to the coronavirus, among other issues (Woody, 2020). The budget was cut after the 2008 economic crisis, but that did not halt the funding for long. Therefore, as can be seen in 2019 and 2020, the budget has been over one trillion dollars in just two years. Yet, the country is always scrounging to find funding for education, healthcare, infrastructure, social services, policing, and emergency management. Policy recommendations have already been proposed in this book on those issues, because the social ramifications of focusing on defense, and foreign conflict, instead of the citizenry of the US are obvious. The point still remains, though, that the House of Representatives, the Senate, and the past three presidents have continued this pattern of funding endless wars with ragtag militias and not countries which pose an existential threat.

In Libya, Somalia, Afghanistan, Iran, and many countries in the Middle East and South America, the US is actively engaged in combat or covert operations to stop (or support) political rebellion groups and eliminate terror cells or various militias in those countries. The US is spending billions of dollars to amass information via drones, submarines, satellites, and intelligence on the ground, and most of the information is regarding threats to local areas.

At this point, most attacks are coming from unmanned aircraft, like a predator drone, and the bombings kill a prominent leader in a particular group and others in the nearby vicinity. And, as Arkin stated in the quote at the beginning of this chapter, these strikes and the ongoing conflicts are allegedly to prevent another terrorist attack on US soil.

That is not the case, however, because if all of the intelligence was collected, and drones were used solely to collect information about threats, then these threats would be known about with no large-scale attacks needed. If someone were concocting a plan to attack the US, they would most likely be eliminated in a timely manner. As well, as will be discussed after this section, the major terroristic threats to the US are "homegrown." With better planning, more soldiers could be in the reserve, or on a domestic base, to protect their homeland instead of being involved in endless skirmishes around the planet. They are endless because there will always be another person to fill the role in a militia that does not have much power, and because the US does not fully understand the politics, religious sentiments, or cultural ideologies that embolden these groups. The mission is not to understand them and neutralize them with a peace treaty or a pact; the mission is to kill or befriend. If that is how the US is viewed by these groups, and we view them as an endless threat requiring action, then this will always be a cycle that calls for more funds. Instead of a problem that the country, the UN, and policing efforts to freeze funds to terrorist organizations could solve.

War has changed because it seeks out the enemy rather than the enemy presenting itself as a force with which to be reckoned. War has changed because it has become a machine of omniscience, having digital blueprints of entire countries and databases of militants on file, while still only attacking fringe mercenaries with no designs on the United States. As stated before, even if they did have nefarious plans, with enough information, they could easily be eliminated once the plan is imminent without a war. Likewise, many countries could handle these issues with UN involvement and typical policing methods. Furthermore, there is a reason why NATO exists, and why the US has many allies in the Middle East. But let us talk about a few of those allies in particular.

Saudi Arabia is the nation where most of the men from the 9/11 attack came from, and a large amount of funding for ISIS comes from various political actors in Saudi Arabia. The Clinton Wikileaks affair, in which Julian Assange released classified documents obtained from the US State Department about US intelligence knowing that Qataris and Saudi Arabians fund ISIS, was an alarming revelation to political analysts at the time (Breitweiser, 2016; Samuels, 2016; Windrem, 2014). The Obama Administration just shrugged it off, and the Trump Administration regularly praises dictators, so not much surprise at the highest levels. The identity of a majority of the donors remains a mystery at this time, but Saudi Prince Bandar bin Sultan has been proven to be a benefactor of ISIS (Geller, 2020). Iraqi Prime Minister Nouri al-Maliki stated that he knows US allies in the Middle East fund ISIS, but various intelligence agencies cannot or will not release a dossier of names (Clemons, 2014). The speculation is that many of the funds from "Angel Investors," as former NATO Supreme Allied Commander James Stavridis called them, are funneled through fundraising events and bank accounts in neighboring countries (Windrem, 2014). Stavridis believed Qataris to be more significant donors than Saudi Arabians.

ISIS makes the majority of their money from oil smuggling in Iraq to other countries, among other illicit trades like selling antique artifacts on the black market (Clemons, 2014; Kenner, 2019). Russian intelligence levelled a damning allegation against Turkey, stating that Erdogan, his son-in-law, and his son facilitate the channeling of ISIS oil which comes from Iraq and Syria into their country (Al-Othman, 2016; Valori, 2015; Zero Hedge, 2015). The accused chain of events is essentially that Turkey wants cheap oil smuggled by ISIS, and this happens through companies and government sectors of Erdogan's government and family, and they support ISIS due to their need for oil and their disdain of the Kurds. As well, and even Vice President Joe Biden stated this at an event at Harvard University, Turkey had given hundreds of millions of dollars in funds and arms to militant groups to attack the Assad regime in Syria (Clemons, 2014; Dickey, 2017; Geller, 2020).

So, as has been demonstrated, many US and NATO allies have funded the very terrorist organizations that the "democratized" nations purport to oppose. Some nations perhaps do oppose terror cells because they indiscriminately rape, murder, and threaten to acquire territory and disseminate their hate-filled religious ideology. Many nations have seemingly been ambivalent, or double agents, which is simple opportunism that has been noted in US affairs as well. And speaking of the US role in propping up friendly governments and actors, the US was also opposed to the Assad regime because of his ties to Russia and China.

A declassified Defense Intelligence Agency (DIA) report, obtained by Judicial Watch in a federal lawsuit, enumerates how ISIS was seen as an asset in toppling the Assad regime while also being an excellent target; hence, the Pentagon justified duplicitous military presence in Syria (Durden, 2015). This is the epitome of realpolitik and military-industrial complex activities: wanting oil pipeline access in Syria/Iraq, selling weapons to allies, and supporting alleged enemies in what has been called a "proxy war" between the "West" and the "East" (Dickey, 2017; Durden, 2015; Geller, 2020). The true goals are territory, resources, funding, and the proliferation of neoliberal capitalism as opposed to old communist enemies. As shown in other case studies, the Imperial-Industrial Complex relies on any means necessary to achieve global business, political and military goals.

Perpetual war is necessary for the Imperial-Industrial Complex as well as the smaller Military-Industrial Complex. As mentioned, the US DOD budget is immense, so much so that it is 38 percent of the world's military budget—being an amount which is larger than the next nine countries on the list of top ten defense spenders combined (Woody, 2020). That includes our Communist nemeses from the days of yore, China and Russia, who spend meager amounts compared to the US while having quite massive GDPs. Once again, related to having military bases in eighty countries around the globe, some of the funding continues the tradition of keeping "Communism in check" by patrolling and policing the world. An additional level of the system entails supporting rebellion and militia groups to further political and business goals for the Empire and its allies. ISIS is defeated as a military group at this time, but the funding to high-profile leaders of the group continues, and the pattern would make one believe that they will have a "flare up" when another Capitalist/Communist fringe-country in the Middle East is having a revolution. DOD, DIA, CIA, and Presidential Cabinet members do not want the incessant destabilization, revolution, and neo-colonization trend to cease.

The Effects at Home: The USA Freedom Act and the War-Profiteers
The USA Freedom Act of 2015, previously known as the USA Patriot Act of 2001, has been the domestic arm of the "War on Terror," and the provisions therein have allowed the FBI, CIA, NSA, ICE, Homeland Security, Congress, Federal Judges and Supreme Court Justices to routinely violate, or uphold violations of, the Constitution of the United States. When the act was an infant

in the early 2000s, there was a harkening to Civil Liberties violations that were committed in the 1960s and 1970s. The Patriot Act was reauthorized several times by the time Congress, during the era of President Obama, revamped this Act with a few constitutionality safeguards and the new name. While there have been thwarted attacks on US soil, which were almost all planned by domestic, not foreign, terrorists, this Act and its predecessor have legitimized the ideology of the "War on Terror," giving unprecedented power to federal law enforcement while foiling plans that could have been deterred with traditional and extant laws and police powers. Furthermore, these laws have allowed the sweeping powers to be used in ways which target innocent people, collect virtually anyone's data in violation of the Fourth Amendment to the Constitution, and the citizens of the United States have been put in a state of perpetual panic when the counterterrorism community knows that almost all of the threats are domestic, not foreign.

To begin with, when it is said that the FBI and the CIA were involved in civil liberties violations in the 1960s and 1970s, that is not speculation. The 1976 Select Committee to Study Governmental Operations with Respect to Intelligence Activities of the United States Senate, which was made public record, displays the ubiquitous nature of the surveillance and insurgent tactics being used against activists during the civil rights movement. Any group, ranging from student bodies to Martin Luther King Junior's March on Washington, was subject to scrutiny by the FBI, CIA, and NSA. In addition, a campaign to read millions of letters and telegrams in the United States, in the name of anti-communism, happened with regularity in the 1960s and 1970s. The Committee Report indicated that letters were opened and photographed by the FBI and CIA, three hundred thousand individuals were indexed into a CIA computer for their operation CHAOS, the NSA collected millions of copies of telegrams from 1947–1975, United States Army Intelligence had files created for an estimated one hundred thousand Americans, and at least twenty-six thousand people were catalogued to be detained in the event of a national emergency (US Senate, 1976).

The Committee Report further indicated that any Black Liberation group, from the Black Panthers to the peaceful civil rights movement, were to be infiltrated, discredited, disbanded, and effectively eliminated. The FBI had a specific directive regarding MLK, which was to "neutralize" him as an effective civil rights leader. In the words of the man in charge of the FBI's "war" against

Dr. King, "No holds were barred"" (US Senate, 1976). The FBI's program was called "counterintelligence program," or COINTELPRO, and it ran the gamut from low-level pranks to high-order conspiracy. Many letters were sent to potential dissidents' spouses to insinuate that an affair was occurring, and misinformation was used by sending death threats, or confirmation that someone was a government informant, to various political actors to make them suspect betrayal in their groups. Wiretaps occurred on anyone who seemed to be a "sympathizer" with Communist leanings, and agents were sent to any large event from welfare protests to any Black Student Union or "New Left" student demonstrations. Presidents Eisenhower, Kennedy, Johnson, and Nixon used intelligence agents to spy on members of Congress and Supreme Court Justices, among many others (US Senate, 1976).

The Cold War, and the paranoia created by a Superpower's need to control the status quo, created an atmosphere rife with civil rights violations in the US. The 1960s were notably tense and politically volatile; the decade included the assassinations of JFK, Malcom X, MLK, and several other reputable politicians or activists. It is not clear if US intelligence agencies were involved in these assassinations (even when President Trump had JFK documents released, they were so heavily redacted they were nigh unreadable), but what is clear is the espionage and infiltration in political movements and neighborhoods alike. Either because of the citizens' desire for revolution or just because someone was behaving in a way which defied norms and social controls. Thus, it is a historical pattern that US intelligence agents are routinely violating the First and Fourth Amendment rights of its citizens with these covert operations and surveillance schemes. These activities occur every year, and in the 21st century, it only intensified.

The USA Freedom Act (USAFA), and its predecessor, the Patriot Act, have been an extension of the "Big Brother" idea of constant surveillance to protect the homeland, but the USAFA has not helped in the apprehension of terrorists compared to the techniques employed by intelligence agencies before the Acts were passed. "The Justice Department's Inspector General's report, released a few weeks prior to the USA FREEDOM Act's authorization vote in Congress...noted that the majority of interviews conducted with FBI agents, 'did not identify any major case developments that resulted from use of the records obtained in response to Section 215 orders'" (Landau and Lubin, 2020). Sections 215 and 702 were sections of the Patriot Act which allowed the mass collection of data in an indiscriminate and ubiquitous fashion—from investigative sources or from telecommunication companies. The "bulk collection" was amended once the Bill became the USAFA in 2015, and it simply made the NSA and FBI go through a judicial application process (Landau and Lubin, 2020). Honestly, authorities do not even need the provisions outlined in the USAFA.

The FBI and NSA have many investigative tools at their disposal, such as information from agencies like TSA or DEA, local law enforcement or inter-disciplinary collaboration, traditional stakeouts, camera recordings, wiretaps, internet surveillance, and access to phone and bank records per Supreme Court decisions over the past forty-two years (Kadidal, 2015). A disturbing trend that has been seen in the realm of criminal investigations is the use of Stingray and Hailstorm machines. These machines are "cell-site simulators" which act like a cell phone tower and consume transmitted metadata from a user's cellular device, including location and, with "augmenters," every detail of the com-munications (ACLU, 2018; Woolf, 2016). These devices are being used with regularity by federal, state, and local authorities in over half of the states in the US (ACLU, 2018). Additionally, law enforcement can, with a warrant and an application process online, request transcripts and user data from Amazon Echo devices and even Amazon web services contract information; a similar process exists for Google, Twitter, and Facebook (Whittaker, 2020). There have been glitches where these websites have allowed anyone with an email to request data of this nature (Whittaker, 2020).

People are being spied on, and with spying, there is the potential for in-formation to be taken out of context, used in court unlawfully, or utilized to demonize a target. According to experts, there is some merit to the 702 section of the USAFA, but generally, law enforcement already has everything needed to investigate potential terrorists. The American Civil Liberties Union (ACLU), and a libertarian group, in separate lawsuits, were awarded rulings by federal judges which stated that the Section 215 collection of data was an unconstitutional breach of privacy (Landau and Lubin, 2020; Kadidal, 2015). Therefore, the USAFA is posing Constitutional problems, and it is almost un-necessary from an investigative standpoint. As well, as it turns out, foreign groups in need of extensive surveillance are not the main enemy in the home-land—terrorists in the US are generally sole perpetrators.

Counterterrorism expert Christopher Wright reported that between 2003–2017, terrorism is almost always carried out on US soil by lone wolves

(Landau and Lubin, 2020). There were no handlers, no affiliations, and no direct ties to terrorist organizations in the Middle East or elsewhere. The important sections of the aforementioned Acts, to the intelligence community, have been rendered ineffective in the US because the actors in terror plots in the US are very often *acting alone*. There has not been much terror-related data to collect because the offenders on the US home turf are not calling or contacting anyone about their individualistic, yet perhaps inspired-by-groups, plans.

As FBI director Christopher Wray stated in a 2018 Senate Committee on Homeland Security and Governmental Affairs:

> The FBI assesses HVEs [homegrown violent extremists] are the greatest terrorism threat to the Homeland. These individuals are global jihad-inspired individuals who are in the U.S., have been radicalized primarily in the U.S., and are not receiving individualized directions from FTOs [foreign terrorist organizations]... This is a significant transformation from the terrorist threat our Nation faced a decade ago (Landau and Lubin, 2020).

Since 2014, in the US, there have been eight deadly terrorism attacks that were inspired by, not orchestrated or directed by, terrorist groups around the globe (Landau and Lubin, 2020). A report from the Heritage Foundation observed that fifty terrorism plans had been foiled in the US from 2001–2012 (Carafano, 2012). That number is naturally higher at the time of this writing, but the fact remains that these would-be terrorists are still generally unaffiliated with foreign interests. There have been a few which were found to be related to al-Qaeda, the Taliban, or ISIS, such as the Lackawanna Six. Khalid Sheikh Mohammed, an officer for Osama bin Laden who was an architect of many successful and unsuccessful international attacks, was found in Pakistan and brought to Guantanamo Bay (Carafano, 2012). Khalid was incarcerated for events that took place by his command, such as claiming he helped plan 9/11, but he did not have further designs on the US that could be proven; as has been seen with serial killers and terrorists, they claim responsibility for actions they did not commit to appear as diabolical and ingenious as possible in order to have a grandiose stature of infamy in history. Khalid is an outlier in the sense of modern terrorism in the US, and he is not connected to the broader phenomenon of homegrown radicals in the US heartland.

Otherwise, there is one profile of assailant which consistently plagues the people in the United States of America: the mass shooter. From California to Florida, and everywhere in between, there are attacks by gunmen who act alone and rack up a grim death toll. The profile can vary, but they are almost always flying solo. These men take automatic weapons and kill anywhere from three to sixty people in just a few minutes. The rationale behind the murders is somewhat unique to the perpetrator; however, the common threads are typically raw anger and hate. This particular murderous mentality is self-righteous, and usually self-serving, and the motives range from being unloved, unsexed, bullied, depressed, isolated, ostracized, or to serve an ideological function. The ideologies can come from religion or personal philosophy and mainly focus on eliminating those whom the shooter has deemed impure: the unholy, the perverted, the infidels, the elite, and the racially inferior are examples of the groups that the mass shooter will fixate on to exact his anger at the world for perceived injustices and inequalities in his own personal delusion. Very often, even though these are quite publicized events, these men are not called terrorists and neither are funding and resources being used to address the problem from a prevention-based platform.

Mass shootings come in two varieties in the US: public domain and school shootings. President Obama mandated that mass shootings be considered an event in which three people are killed by gunfire (Wilson, 2019). The majority of school shootings are not mass shootings. According to analyses conducted by NBC and CNN, there have been 185 school shootings since 2009, with 378 victims (119 deaths and 259 injuries) (Chiwaya et al, 2018; Walker et al, 2019). The high-profile mass shootings were Sandy Hook Elementary in Connecticut, Marjory Stoneman Douglas High School in Florida, and Santa Fe High School in Texas. The former occurred in 2012, and the latter two occurred in 2018. All three had casualties higher than ten, and Sandy Hook had twenty-six fatalities. Nonetheless, however, and this is not to diminish the damage done at the schools, the mass shootings in the US which are perpetrated by older men create a higher body count.

The group *Mother Jones* compiled a list of mass shootings based on Obama's definition since the year 1982. In the database, the records reflect that there have been 114 mass shooting events, 942 people have been murdered, and 1,406 have been injured (Wilson, 2019). In 2019 there were two highly publicized shootings, the Walmart in El Paso, Texas, and the Dayton,

Ohio, bar scene, because both happened over the same weekend and thirty-one lives were lost. In 2016 and 2017 the carnage was more devastating than in the public's recent memories, because we all witnessed the aftermath of the Pulse Nightclub and Las Vegas mass shootings. Omar Mateen killed forty-nine people in Orlando at the club, and Stephen Paddock killed sixty and injured over four hundred in the chaos that was Las Vegas that night. A comprehensive list is not possible within the scope of this book, but the pertinent fact for our purposes is that men like these are almost never labeled terrorists. The school shooters are not labeled terrorists. However, as the FBI indicated, the terrorists who are effective and active in the US are not linked to international organizations; they are homegrown violent extremists (HVEs).

The Department of Homeland Security (DHS) has labeled domestic terrorism as the top terror-related threat to the US. They have also enumerated subsections of priorities and threat levels. DHS's State of the Homeland Threat Assessment 2020 has announced that white supremacist groups, who fall under the category of domestic violent extremists, are the most lethal. The report stated: "Among DVE [domestic violent extremist] actors, WSEs [white supremacist extremists] conducted half of all lethal attacks (8 of 16), resulting in the majority of deaths (39 of 48)" (Swan, 2020).

At this point, DHS and the Justice Department are looking into the possibility of adding ANTIFA, the left-leaning semi-militant group, to its list, but at this time, it has not made it into the Threat Assessment (Swan, 2020). One thing that is different about the past few years is that we are now seeing homegrown extremist groups instead of individuals, and these groups have an animus of anti-equality and anti-government sentiments. As well, a growing issue is that these groups see themselves as emboldened freedom fighters fighting a radical liberal order which will turn our country into a "socialist" country, and they very often have the support of Donald Trump, the current President of the United States. Regarding the protests and tangential riots related to police brutality and social justice in the US in 2020, Trump "has repeatedly threatened protesters with mayhem or murder. Trump has also told governors to 'dominate' the protesters and has said that he may invoke the Insurrection Act, which dates to the early 19th century and has rarely been used," and "Trump has also ordered his paramilitary forces — both the police and other law enforcement officers as well as his 'MAGA Army' of thugs — to put down the protests and the people's uprising" (Devega, 2020).

What must be noted is that riots do need to be pacified because of two important reasons: they destroy neighborhoods of plenty of people who support peaceful activism, and they pose a true risk of harm to many civilians. Peaceful protests are an obvious 1st Amendment right. However, the feature of interest in the above quotes is the alarming fact that the president is siding with the groups which his DHS has claimed to be the most lethal form of terrorism on US soil. Notwithstanding that the author believes mass shooters need to be included in the concept of terrorism for prevention and criminal labeling reasons. Furthermore, it was USAFA privileges that allowed federal law enforcement to anonymously detain protesters in cities like Portland, Oregon, in 2020, because the USAFA can suspend due process if you are perceived to be a threat to national security. Even though they were clearly looking for the ring leaders in these protests, in which portions devolved into riots, why did they use these Kremlin-esque tactics? Why did they not just use their ability to track and surveil people on the internet, and through cell phone data, to find the movement leaders? Was it simply to scare the protesters, or was it a show of force that has not been publicly witnessed and acknowledged since the 1960s and 1970s? It is not clear at this time, and what also remains obfuscated is the identity of the agency which detained these people; we do not know if it was NSA, CIA, DHS, or FBI. But it was one of them.

What has been made clear is that the NSA and DHS cannot continue to promise us that a foreign group of terrorists is imminently preparing an attack on US soil. The real threat has been, and perhaps always has been, domestic extremists. These people have traditionally been lone wolves, but the DHS has admitted that there is a surge of domestic terrorists in the form of white supremacist groups. Current White House officials have consistently avoided talks with DHS about labeling these groups "terrorists" (Swan, 2020). This labeling problem has lasted for many years. Domestic terrorists such as Timothy McVeigh or Ted Kaczynski have earned the title and are either dead or sitting in the Florence ADX Supermax prison in Colorado. Florence ADX and Guantanamo Bay house the men connected to 9/11 as well.

Once you get the label of "terrorist," you will receive the same level of authority, including surveillance of proper targets and jailing them in maximum security prisons, regardless of ideology or creed. But every other form of terrorist in the US, except the Islamic-Jihad international terror cells which are virtually inactive in the US, do not receive the label because it would make the "War on Terror" seem illegitimate. Our Intelligence agencies have even euphemized the main threat as "homegrown/domestic violent extremists"—not terrorists. The Intelligence agencies in our nation do not receive anywhere near the amount of funding that the DOD receives, and so they definitely needed to maintain the illusion that they are preventing foreign operations to consistently be awarded funding for their ostensibly utilitarian services. It seems as if they are becoming more practical and honest as the majority of intelligence agencies, excluding the CIA, become more transparent. However, they have claimed for years that they were fighting a threat that was not there while allowing Russians to interfere with our elections and China to infiltrate our universities. It seems as if the Communist parties simply have to use party tricks, like donating or using the internet, to dupe sophisticated pillars of US society.

Funding as an impetus for secrecy and corruption is seen across the board in the broad field of foreign and domestic Defense. Regarding the Military-Industrial Complex, we see the problems of monopoly, poor wealth distribution, private-contractor incompetence, security, corruption, and fraud become intertwined in a microcosm of all the problems regarding global-imperialism. One major problem with the Defense sector, including Intelligence agencies in this issue, is private contracting. As has been noted in this chapter already, private contractors in Iraq were the direct effect, and subsequent beneficiaries, of high-order corruption in the White House. Aside from Halliburton and KBR's corporate greed and war-profiteering from oil and post-war reconstruction, other companies have displayed this deviant and negative side of capitalism. What is ironic is that so much of the efforts around the globe are for capitalistic gain, but so much of the work that is done by for-profit contractors is paid for by American taxes.

As paraphrased from Deborah Avant, a Military-Industrial Complex expert, "the government's willingness to contract with a few cowboy companies like Aegis - a U.K.-based firm whose infamous founder and CEO Tim Spicer was implicated for breaking an arms embargo in Sierra Leone - only reinforces the fear that U.S. foreign policy is being outsourced to corporate 'mercenaries'" (Cray, 2006). Aegis is a private security firm, and there are many around the world that have connections to intelligence agencies, warlords, cartels, and wealthy businessmen alike, just as the CIA does. The CIA also outsources much of their labor, to the tune of half of their budget (Cray, 2006). Intelligence operations at Abu Ghraib, the infamous prison where human rights abuses like torture took place, were largely performed by outsourced companies like CACI and Titan.

CACI was eventually sued in the US for Constitutional violations, like the 8th Amendment, by the Center for Constitutional Rights in the Federal Court for the District of Columbia (Cray, 2006). CACI was found innocent by a jury in that case, but they stopped doing a lot of contracting. Titan, on the other hand, paid $28.5 million for violating the Foreign Corrupt Practices Act for the torture and possessing classified information—then they were bought by L-3 and became the largest corporate-intelligence company in the world which continues to be granted army contracts (Cray, 2006).

KBR, the Halliburton subsidiary, had a civil lawsuit filed against them by the Department of Justice for "overbilling" and the Defense Contractors Audit Agency had recommended cutting them off from millions in funding—but still, they usually got their contract fulfilled (Holan, 2010). The multi-million-dollar company KBR, which had received millions of dollars in government contracts, only ended up paying the United States a whopping $108,342.10 for violating the Anti-Kickback Act (justice.gov). However, this is an overarching theme within the world of PMCs, or private military contractors, that they can be corrupt on the taxpayer's dime, and there are not many laws to penalize them for malfeasance; or they just get off with a slap on the wrist. The Commission on Wartime Contracting in Iraq and Afghanistan stated that "the level of corruption by defense contractors may be as high as $60 billion" (Young, 2013).

Companies like Lockheed Martin and Boeing, which have made the most money off of military contracts over the years, consistently lobby for more Defense spending and Bills which engender the state of perpetual war. The Center for Responsive Politics has an impressive database which tracks the lobbying and contributions of all major corporations and investors of US political parties. Lockheed Martin regularly contributes to both major political parties, at rates that are over four million dollas combined since 2012, and they have spent over ten million dollars in lobbying efforts for Defense spending annually since 2007 (CRP, 2020; Dane, 2015). The trend is similar with Boeing, Northrop Grumman, and General Dynamics. It should not surprise anyone that both sides of the political aisle have contributions given by war-profiteers; it is simply business in their eyes. And duality is much more beneficial, as was described earlier in this text, in regard to the circumstances of Saddam Hussein and ISIS being allies of convenience, until they are not. This is also true in the numerous scenarios of the CIA supporting coups and dictators when necessary. And of course, our allies such as Saudi Arabia, Turkey, Israel, and Egypt will always be exonerated in the American Court of Public Opinion.

One more story of such duality will serve us well before getting to the conclusion of this chapter. Now, duplicity in war-profiteering, and militaristic hedonism, are the name of the game. The US sends approximately ten billion dollars in military equipment, on average, to nearly one hundred countries every year (Sauter and Stebbins, 2017). This continues the cycle of weapons being channeled to groups who are enemies in one country but allies in another. The enemy of my enemy is my friend, and anyone willing to buy weapons and planes is a friend anyway. The story of Viktor Bout is another shining example of "ally of convenience" and scapegoat. Viktor Bout was a notorious international arms dealer, sometimes referred to as the "Merchant of Death." Viktor made most of his money funding both sides of wars in Africa, and the UN and many international bodies recognized him as a dangerous man who needed to be brought to justice. During the Iraq War, Viktor was flying in weapons and supplies for the US military (Daly, 2004).

As Daly (2004) put it:

> [the US] used Bout to ferry arms shipments to the northern Alliance for its operations against the Taliban. In 2004, the Bush administration began to press for Bout to be left off planned UN sanctions, in spite of French efforts at the UN in March 2004 to freeze his assets and an outstanding Interpol warrant for his arrest. A senior Western diplomat aware of the issues said, 'We are disgusted that Bout won't be on the list, even though he is the principal arms dealer in the region. If we want peace in that region, it seems evident that he should be on that list.' The Bush administration pressured the Blair government to remove Bout from its preliminary list of individuals for inclusion, and this was duly noted. Washington's logic is that Bout should be dealt with by separate UN measures dealing specifically with arms dealers. In the final analysis, Bout is able to operate freely for two simple

reasons: he provides a service and is discreet, operating through his many front companies.

Once more military press was in the mainstream media during the Iraq War, the US turned Viktor Bout into a scapegoat, which was mutually supported by many governments around the world due to Bout's history of illegal arms trafficking. Viktor was entrapped and tricked in a DEA sting in Bangkok, Thailand, believing that he was making deals with the Colombian guerilla group FARC, and he was swiftly extradited from Thailand to the US where he currently sits in prison after he was convicted of many crimes (CNN, 2012). Therefore, in the realm of realpolitik, the maxim is to take what you can and let no one take it from you. With geopolitics, however, if you are not a government, you will not have the sovereignty, which can exempt you from common law.

Another theme throughout the Military-Industrial complex is the revolving door. The revolving door of government personnel becoming well-networked professionals in the industry in question, after they have served their government term, and vice versa regarding private sector professionals becoming government employees, has a longstanding tradition of creating conflicts of interest and general nepotism. With almost every company which provides the government with fighter jets, missiles, tanks, naval vessels, armor, and miscellaneous equipment and gear, over half of the lobbyists were previously government employees (Dane, 2015). This was indicated in a previous chapter regarding various Federal Government Appointees being chosen for a Secretary or Chief position due to being a CEO or well-respected entrepreneur in the particular industry (environment, energy, defense, finance, and so on). Lastly, either before or after they work for the government, CEOs in Defense are paid millions of dollars every year, which is consistent with every other brand of globalizing monopolies. These corporations are doling out massive bonuses and salary increases to a few men rather than spreading the wealth more proportionately to engineers, assembly line workers, and everyone in the hierarchy of the corporation.

As Smedley D. Butler, a US Marine Corps Major General who served in WWI, stated:

> War is a racket. It always has been. It is possibly the oldest, easily the most profitable, surely the most vicious. It is the

> only one international in scope. It is the only one in which
> the profits are reckoned in dollars and the losses in lives. A
> racket is best described, I believe, as something that is not
> what it seems to the majority of the people. Only a small 'in-
> side' group knows what it is about. It is conducted for the
> benefit of the very few, at the expense of the very many. Out
> of war a few people make huge fortunes (Dane, 2015).

Luckily for him, Smedley did not have to see the eventual proliferation of international rackets, from certain Non-Profits and shell corporations, to international pyramid schemes, government contractors, and illegal and inhumane business practices and materials sourcing. However, in his day and age, it was most likely correct that war was the only international racket. To this very day, it still can be, and it is with regularity. War is often tied up in so much scandal and realpolitik, be it resource related, to prop up a puppet government, to punish Communists, or to enrich the elite and the oligarchic republic. Truthfully, many politicians and professionals involved in the Military-Industrial Complex do not even care about the purpose behind the wars or the issues that arise in the homeland because they make exorbitant amounts of money from war. They will pretend to care about the issues people usually tout when they babble rhetoric about modern warfare such as "peacekeeping," "national security," "democratizing," "liberation," "terrorism," and "Communism." These ideologies, in practice, have been debunked, for the most part, as moral panic, social engineering, self-preservation, and opportunism in this chapter.

The policy recommendations which come forth out of this "War on Terror" study are as follows:

#1: Ratify the Rome Statute of the International Criminal Court

#2: On a foreign policy and military level, reduce the number of troops in unnecessary conflicts, and the amount of military equipment being made, to be able to reallocate portions of DOD funds to other sectors of the government (Health and Human Services, Department of Education, Environmental Protection Agency, the United States Postal Service, and so many others).

#3: Prioritize diplomacy and the use of NATO in international affairs.

#4: Limit private contract outsourcing of reconstruction efforts and private security in war. This concept is not probable with regard to machines and arms, but for reconstruction and private security, this is very possible. Use groups like the Defense Contract Audit Association and Government Accountability Office, coupled with the Department of Justice and Military Intelligence, to properly screen private contractors for past incompetence or fraud, conflicts of interest, or general ineligibility based on factors these institutions find prudent.

#5: Eliminate unconstitutional sections of the USA Freedom Act.

#6: Label mass shooters and homegrown violent extremists as terrorists. Be transparent about the efficacy of the original intentions of the "War on Terror" and about the real nature of Homeland Security threats.

#7: Close Guantanamo Bay, because we have prisons in the United States that can handle the incarcerated terrorist population. Simultaneously, focus on releasing people from federal prisons that do not belong there (i.e., for drug crimes from the 1980s and 1990s) while inserting terrorists from Guantanamo Bay, and domestic terrorists, into US prisons. This will also allow for transparency regarding humane treatment of prisoners.

Chapter 7:

The New Machiavelli and the Rules of the Game of Power

"The Romans, in the provinces which they conquered, were careful to fulfill these requirements: they sent out colonies, they treated the weaker favorably without letting their powers increase, they weakened the powerful, and they did not allow powerful aliens to gain any standing there."
~ Niccolo Machiavelli in *The Prince*

This book has, at this point, attempted to be what its subtitle stated: an exploration of the relationship between democracy, necessary evils, corruption, and realpolitik. The synthesis of all of these topics leads to the concepts of American Empire, or what has now been coined as the Imperial-Industrial Complex in this text. The timeline of a Superpower dominating the world after a devastating war was vital to understanding the evolution of an Empire. After WWII, the world was split between two competing philosophies of economy and governance, capitalism and communism, and from this great trauma came the belief that the US needed to be a global military to ensure peace. Then, American businesses started to occupy foreign spaces while leaving their fellow Americans to struggle for jobs in the most unequal and impoverished developed nation.

In reality, the US, the UK, Russia, and China have only built upon the colonization that was left in shambles after the two World Wars—they were not the first to conquer foreign lands through hard or soft power. However, in this web of fear and competition for ultra-sovereignty, the US has always been able to "fight fire with fire" in the sense that it will revert to corrupt covert operations to maintain its power, just as the "enemy" does. Everyone knows that there were millions killed in Russian labor camps and Mao Zedong's "Great Leap Forward" initiative in China, and that many elements of Communism, compounded with the atrocities of the Holocaust, terrified the world of the depths of human depravity, in governance particularly. But why did the notion of peacekeeping devolve into a notion of hegemony?

After the military finished its campaign in Vietnam, we should have taken a break from "destroying communism." But during the Cold War of the 1950s–1980s, the US became so paranoid that its intelligence agencies were acting like the Gestapo—spying on its own citizens while masterminding the murders of government leaders in Iraq, the Democratic Republic of Congo, Chile, Nicaragua, Cuba, and other supporters of Communism. This governmental prerogative, coupled with the notion that American commerce would "save the world from the evils of Communism," kickstarted a complex global financial system reliant on endless debt and production. This financial system, supported by international trade laws, establishes laissez-faire trading as more important than safe, humane, and regulated business, just as the US "global mission" believes that expansionism is more important than taking care of its own citizens.

When there are unchecked powers in the face of fear, there is also unchecked corruption from the top down. What has been seen with regard to the US hierarchy, and neo-colonization, is that the White House, the Pentagon, the CIA, the State Department, and corporations know the volume of resources and untapped potential in so many nations of the Earth—and with our influence and might, we could have cheap access to all of it, from oil and metals to food and lumber. The US did not need to conquer territories in this new age, it simply needed to assess the "threat" and "risk" levels of any given nation, in association with the rewards of a relationship, for a cost-benefit analysis that would indicate the ways in which the US could compel a nation to become a partner in this neoliberal fetishization of profit margins. And other times, the relationship already existed, or others were simply invited (i.e. NAFTA and TPP). The political economy had become the second-most important piece to defeating Communism, right after old-fashioned armies.

One thing that is interesting about the tactics of creating puppet governments, or forging alliances, for the mutual benefit of entire nations or for a few powerful characters is that it is not new at all. The tactics of mutually assured benefit or destruction have been used by kings, armies, rivals, and blackmailers of all sorts since the beginnings of civilization. Very often, the peace would be brokered by pragmatics and individual gain, such as arranging a marriage between two royal adolescents. These bargaining chips, which came in the form of two naïve juveniles, ensured an alliance between two kingdoms while also establishing the promise of trade between the nations for food, linens, metals, general goods, and traveling artisans and craftsmen. For some nations throughout time, this was a lifeline, for others, it was a gold mine.

What became necessary in the evolution of realpolitik was the ability to understand the ways in which the land in other countries legitimized the right to rule by way of the people's support. If a ruler lost important relations with a nation which supplied wheat, for example, the people may revolt. If a trade route was lost, and the people lost their ability to access staples like salt, potatoes or apples, iron ore, or fish, then there could easily be a call to arms or uprising. What is paramount for the ruler is to ensure the people that the problem lies with the enemy, and for whatever reason, the enemy needs to pay up in one way or another. Many times, the enemy will be a problematic figure in politics instead of another nation. The war psychology of hating the enemy that is inculcated into a soldier presents itself in a sedentary way in politics: polarizing party propaganda. Or more simply, the teaching that "their group is evil, and our group is good, and we need to make sure they have no power." The groups believe this because they also believe in self-righteous Manifest Destiny, which is also part of the group lesson plan.

Max Weber noted something similar in his "Protestant Ethic and the Spirit of Capitalism." To the Protestant people of mainland Europe or the US in the late 1800s into the 1910s, work itself was for the glory of God, Weber indicated, and the industry and primacy of "Christian" nations was Manifest Destiny for God's glory and theirs. When a leader can shift the ideology to encompass the nation's glory too, then we find personal glory and national prestige intertwined. Willing to believe in the efforts of the homeland, or even a group, the young people of nations have been told very ethnocentric ideas over the years in Japan, Russia, China, the US, the UK, France, Germany, and Italy.

Speaking of Italy and using nationalism and patriotism to embolden a large agenda, we can move on to the man mentioned in the title of this chapter: Niccolo Machiavelli. Machiavelli was the person who redefined political science in the Renaissance because he decided to write about what rulers and aristocrats did and how to maintain power regardless of morals and ethics. Machiavelli did believe in the humanity of morals and ethics but also observed that those in power only play by the rules if they are guaranteed to win. His analyses will help to demonstrate how leaders and militaries have been taught the same power plays from an ancient set of tactics, and how the writings of Machiavelli correlate with modern polity.

A few historians throughout time have been able to display an unbiased view on the true accomplishments, failures, and personalities of leaders, but Machiavelli decided to analyze what he saw in Italy, and what he knew of history, to make a political guide for maintaining power. The book of import for our purposes was a treatise to Lorenzo de Medici II, and it was called *The Prince*. Machiavelli told many true stories of power, ranging from quelling civil unrest to managing subjects after a hostile takeover. With Machiavelli's understanding of the Renaissance Zeitgeist, in conjunction with the Rules of the Game of Power which were outlined in chapter three of this book, we shall assess the status of the American Empire and what kind of rule-following and rule-breaking will be required for national homeostasis in the near future.

Fear and Power

First and foremost, it must be stated that *The Prince* was in actuality an academic petition to unify Italy as a Republic. Machiavelli was raised in highly divisive times because, as was mentioned earlier, Italy and Germany were not unified nations until the eighteenth and nineteenth centuries. Sectarianism, independent principalities, city-states of antiquity, invasions, and constant landgrabs were the hallmarks of late fifteenth-century Italian politics. Machiavelli was not a ruthless person who advocated for tyranny or absolute power— he was, simply put, a pragmatist who wanted the aristocracy of the day to stop the French and German invasions, as well as the infighting amongst Princes, Kings, and the Papal Powers of the Borgias. To Machiavelli, certain things were inherently true about human nature, as cynical as it may be. Such as, people are self-serving, people will always reach for power, people are opportunists and will betray you, and people operate based on rewards and punishments, just as the Utilitarian, Jeremy Bentham, believed.

When it comes to questions of power, Machiavelli asked the proverbial questions and usually answered them bluntly. Should a "Prince," or someone with power, choose to be feared or loved? Machiavelli states that "one should like to be both; but since it is difficult to combine the two, it is much safer to be feared than loved, when one has to do without one of the two," (Machiavelli, 2009). After discussing that people are fickle, and that love is a bond which men commonly break, Machiavelli insists that the fear of punishment is stronger than the love of Princes who keep a populace safe, fed, and civil. So, he states:

> A prince ought nevertheless to make himself feared in such a way that, even though he does not win love, he avoids hatred; since it is quite possible to be both feared and yet not hated at the same time; he can always manage this if he keeps his hands off the possessions of his citizens and subjects, and off their womenfolk. And even when he needs to take someone's life, he should do so when there is sufficient justification and a manifest reason (Machiavelli, 2009).

Another proverbial question, and one which was posed at the beginning of this book, is Will absolute power corrupt absolutely? To Machiavelli, yes, all power corrupts, but the corruption must be kept in check by systems of priority and law; and moral corruption is preferred over political corruption. In governance, power is necessary for instilling order to life and society. These themes have arisen in many contexts, even in Nazi Germany, because the people chose excessive power over potential anarchy. When a population is given the choice between the *feelings* of safety and security as opposed to the *feelings* of uncertainty and fear, they will often elect unrestricted powers. Then, fear will be used to make people "get with the program."

To Machiavelli, fear is a more powerful motivator than love. In the US, elected officials thrive off of populations being in fear of the enemy, and afraid of law enforcement. Therefore, by extension, the governor, or senator, or president can be feared instead of loved (but not hated) because of the powers they have over law enforcement. Many US citizens live in fear because of law enforcement either because of a history of hotspot policing and instances of police brutality or because they will silence detractors. When people dissent, they are often silenced if they are in a public place or official proceeding—and this causes many to fear.

US citizens are also afraid of their politicians because of the policies they can enact, and because of their influence with their political bases. Incitement of assembly action, with support of politicians, can lead to street-level violence at volatile mass gatherings. This has happened with both political parties in the US; Skokie, Illinois, and Charlotte, South Carolina, are good, opposite examples. When liberals protest against systemic racism of the police or a particular politician, they will be met with a counterprotest which was either incited by a politician or civilian. When the conservatives rally about 2nd Amendment rights, or against socialized healthcare, they will be met with a counterprotest as well. Conservatives have, more often than liberals, used harassment techniques (at election polling locations and abortion clinics to name a couple places) to declare their disdain. These examples of conflict make people afraid of one another, and of the politicians they support. Nonetheless, fear has definitely mutated in our new age compared to what Machiavelli and his contemporaries witnessed.

As we have explored, the "War on Terror" was an example which demonstrated the majority's fear put into policy. To give another example of a false war based on fear, we will explore the "War on Drugs" for a few paragraphs. These "wars" were exercises of hard power to legitimize the government, win favor for US politicians, and calm the panic of the people. As was shown in the previous chapter, the "War on Terror" was fraudulent because the enemy is never who those in Defense say it is (Iraq had nothing to do with 9/11, and the main terrorist threat to the homeland is domestic terrorists), and military powers have been used to further an agenda of privatizing oil and fighting Communism. What will be demonstrated shortly, is that the "War on Drugs" was fraught with corruption and is interwoven into a governmental scandal we have already covered: the Iran-Contra affair.

The War on Drugs began with Nixon and the Racketeering-Influenced and Corrupt Organizations (RICO) laws, but truly, this "war" hit its stride in the Reagan and Clinton Administrations. The pattern of Intelligence agencies acting as paramilitaries or counterinsurgencies in the US, and across the globe, for policy and agenda reasons, is continued in this story. If you recall, from the previous chapter, the Iran-Contra scandal had to do with President Reagan commanding the sale of arms to Iran to pay for US support of the Nicaraguan Contras, an anti-communist militia and cartel. The scandal occurred because the president wanted continued funding for the Contras, to whom Congress had cut off funding by 1985. The CIA was heavily involved in the transmission of information, money, and weapons to the Contras before and during the Iran-Contra affair. A large source of money for the Contras, before and during the Iran-Contra scandal, was cocaine. Most of the money was being used to fund their coup of the Nicaraguan government, and in the early 1980s, the CIA assisted them in their trafficking scheme into Los Angeles at a prolific rate.

Cocaine was transferred from Nicaragua to the US via plane, most of the time. This is because the weapons for Nicaragua were flown by various pilots who would bring cocaine back to the US with permission from the CIA and Oliver North, the National Security Council official in charge of US dealings with the Contras (Grim et al, 2014). Because of articles being published in 1985, and various suspicions, then-Senator John Kerry launched a Congressional Investigation into the CIA's involvement with the Contras and narcotics trafficking. According to the report: "many of the pilots ferrying weapons and supplies south for the CIA were known to have backgrounds in drug trafficking. Kerry's investigation cited SETCO Aviation, the company the U.S. had contracted to handle many of the flights, as an example of CIA complicity in the drug trade. According to a 1983 Customs Service report, SETCO was 'headed by Juan Ramon Matta Ballesteros, a class I DEA violator'" (Grim et al, 2014). Another pilot was William Robert "Tosh" Plumlee, who spoke with then-Senator Gary Hart, who passed on information to John Kerry.

Plumlee told Hart about the routine transports of arms to the Nicaraguan rebels, and cocaine back to the US, with help from the CIA. As Grim et al (2014) put it, "Plumlee flew weapons into Latin America for decades for the CIA. When the Contra revolution took off in the 1980s, Plumlee says he continued to transport arms south for the spy agency and bring cocaine back with him, with the blessing of the U.S. government." Once the plane arrived in California, it was time for transactions. Danilo Blandon and his boss, Norwin Meneses, were the "Kingpins" who would distribute through traffickers like Rick Ross, and from there, it was sold throughout Los Angeles and sections of the Midwest (Grim et al, 2014). The profit margins which were owed to the Contras back in Nicaragua were taken back in cash by Adolfo Carlero, laundered through banks in Florida, or were sent as cash or weapons by CIA operatives (Grim et al, 2014).

The moral panic across the US came from the media portrayal of the street-level circumstances of the War on Drugs. People were using crack-cocaine, there were gang wars, cops received grant money and were driving around in tanks, and politicians spread rhetoric about "generations lost" and the rise of the highly fictitious criminal "Superpredator." The *Washington Post*, the *New York Times*, and criminologists eventually concurred that the epidemic of the 1980s was not one of crack but one of hyperboles (Reinarman and Levine, 2014). Crack-cocaine is not more dangerous than cocaine, and both are nowhere near as dangerous as alcohol and its impact on communities across the US (Reinarman and Levine, 2014). And the general public would not be addicted to, or killed by, crack-cocaine; and gang violence, just like all organized crime, generally affects gang members only, but of course, there can be innocent bystanders or collateral damage.

The War on Drugs failed because it did not stop drug use, it did not halt violent crimes, and it did not thwart overall drug trafficking, as the government proposed it would. Legally, it created a one-hundred-to-one sentencing ratio of crack-cocaine compared to powder cocaine, meaning that someone found with one gram of crack would be sentenced as if they had one hundred grams of cocaine. Only recently was the sentence reduced from one hundred to one to eighteen to one, the calculus of which makes no sense. The War on Drugs led to draconian sentences of forty years, or even life without parole, in prisons for non-violent drug crimes. This War on Drugs was a continuation of race-based fear in drug policies and covert operations of FBI in urban areas. As well, it was a continuation of criminal justice policies which disproportionately affect the black community. From the White House down to mass media, the "crack epidemic" was framed as a National Security threat, whereas cocaine and the recent opioid epidemic have been framed as Public Health emergencies. And, aside from the underworld workings of the CIA, fear is what allowed the War on Drugs and the War on Terror to manifest on a policy level.

Political power is derived from the pleasure of the people because they will be able to eventually oust an unpopular candidate through one channel or another, or over time. But, also, police and military powers are at the disposal of those in political power, and they must punish certain offenders to keep society in line with the status quo. Thus, politicians can be feared because of their policies, agendas, and/or armies of police and national guard. And they can put you in fear to make you need them with excellent messaging and rhetoric. We see this all the time with "tough on crime" politicians, who would not look at the facts about criminal justice on any given day to help change the system, such as with War on Drugs policies. The War on Terror was a problem which was highly mythologized by presidents and administrations both Democrat and Republican. This strategy of demagoguery plays on human nature and instincts, and those in power have learned to use fear to their advantage.

The never-ending US political agenda of anti-communism is always playing out on many levels. Naturally, we have discussed many anti-communism efforts on military and espionage levels, but it happens in garden-variety politics. The smear campaigns which say "they're trying to turn us into a socialist country" makes people afraid and is based on lies. People are afraid of the Gulag, people are afraid of Mao Zedong's Marxism, and yet none of those things are socialism. Communism and socialism are not the same, and many would argue that communism played out very negatively in certain countries, but that was man's corruption of an ideal. We see the same corruption in capitalism, it is just not concentrated entirely in the homeland.

Communism does involve the state controlling nearly every element of life, from business to health services to media, but still they do not control everything. There is some capitalism in communism, and there is a lot of capitalism in democratic socialism. Democratic socialism focuses government control and regulation on what is necessary, tax-funded, and a human right in the country. The US does not have a broad understanding of human rights, even believing that water and healthcare are not human rights. In democratic-socialist nations, the people are guaranteed a social services safety net which can provide basic needs, and healthcare and vocational/college educations are free because they are seen as rights. They are also seen as investments in the future. The US has many elements which are also socialism in action.

What we share in common with socialist nations are our institutions and safety nets which are services to the people. The military, the police, public school systems, social security for the elderly, Medicaid/Medicare for the impoverished or retired, social services which grant supplemental nutrition funds or temporary relief funds to needy families, government subsidies to hospitals or essential industries, stimulus packages, infrastructure funding for roads and utilities, and so many other things are technically socialistic in nature. The United States is a capitalist country which has elements of socialism embedded into it for the betterment of the people. Just as democratic-socialist nations around the world, from Canada to Sweden, have plenty of capitalism. The US is politically mixed in the way that Germany, the UK, and Australia are. Generally, our budgets are mismanaged, and our tax priorities skewed. However, we shall now move on from fear in politics, and misconceptions, and discuss some of the other Machiavellian tenets.

The Principles of Conquest and Governance, or the Prince and His Subjects

As was shown in the quote at the beginning of this chapter, Machiavelli wrote extensively about conquering opponents in *The Prince*. He outlined basic rules for success, and cautionary tales about failure, but the principles he outlined were fairly simple. When conquering a new territory: defeat the enemy on any military front, establish colonies and a few military bases in the land to be conquered, help the weak in the country overthrow their current regime without giving them too much power, destroy the powerful families and institutions who have loyalties and alliances in the nation, and do not allow other invaders or foreigners to get a foothold in the country while it is destabilizing. Essentially, we are talking about total domination, but there is a phased process which relies on covert tactics and psychological warfare as much as it relies on troops and colonization. That topic has been covered extensively in this book, and it will now be discussed in a conceptual format. We have discussed the specifics of how the US finds itself globalized in the form of an empire, but now we can discuss how its operations compare to ancient empires. Let us use a Machiavellian lens to see how the operations of the military, intelligence agencies, and international business of the US compare to Machiavelli's gold standard for imperialism: The Romans.

The US has definitely followed the Machiavellian program. The US was able to become a superpower because of the atrocities and tragedy of WWII, and from there, the Imperial-Industrial Complex started to bloom. Finding a common enemy is perfect for group polarization and invoking hatred, and this works on personal or organizational levels. The common enemy, Communism, was an excellent justification for war and occupation after WWII. The US occupied Japan, and the reconstruction efforts included the introduction of American business and trade into their nation. After that, Korea was an excellent next step. The same thing happened in Korea with regard to occupation. The US was stationed there to defend against North Korea and China and, truly, never left. Through our Machiavellian lens, military occupations, or CIA covert operations and coups, will be considered colonies and paramilitary action.

As has been stated in this text, the US has military bases in eighty countries, and we have used the tactics described as "treating the weaker favorably" and "weakening the powerful" by supporting rebel groups opposed to the authorities in Iraq, Nicaragua, the Democratic Republic of Congo, Chile, and other nations. So, the first few tenets of Machiavelli's conquest strategy have been adhered to. The differences in the modern era come down to the ways in which colonization of foreign lands occurs. Boots on the ground works, but the world and our allies do not agree with war around the globe for explicit imperial purposes. They are, however, fine with covert operations and the insertion of international business, embassies, and military bases in areas which have been assisted by superpowers but no longer require hard power to enforce the agenda of globalized capitalism. This was the way that colonization advanced. In China, India, and African nations, international business and covert operations were the new way to keep the old trade routes and diplomatic networks alive—which were created by true imperial-colonialism in the 1800s.

One nation cannot dominate the entire planet, even though they may try tenaciously to achieve that task. So, in lieu of actual imperialism, which was seen in bygone eras, some areas are simply tied into the agenda without having colonialism affect them. Many nations of the Earth that do not have US military bases and CIA activity, which are part of the global market, still have US factories and companies in them. This is a form of neo-colonialism in which the US still has control of areas which rely on them for work, and have sway in their markets and politics. This is something that did not occur in antiquity, because the production of goods was not outsourced, and if something was beyond an imperial border, trade routes ensured the selling and bartering of necessary goods.

The Romans established Colonial-Prefectures, in which a Governor, for example Pontius Pilate in Judea during the time of Christ, ruled the area with a faction of Roman soldiers. The people still had their own religion, systems of governance and traditions, but the main difference is that they owed Rome taxes, and they were a part of the large network of the Roman Empire. To continue with the example of Judea, the area was rich in olives, incense, fish, salt, and other commodities. Rome ruled it as a principality; the empire shared in the goods, and Judea would make money. The main problems for the Romans were these 1) uprisings against tyranny, 2) exacting law and order when local officials could not, 3) constant regime changes and vying for power, 4) imperial expansion, which, for finances and defense, was unsustainable.

There are many similarities, and differences, between the empires of the US and Rome. We shall now focus our lens on that last problem for the Romans, expansion and unsustainability. The US has a problem with budgeting and focusing too much on expansionism from a business and military standpoint. These errors, which one could call blindsides, created by a quest for global control and profit, are already unsustainable. We have seen that with the national debt, economic bubbles which burst, pollution around the planet, illegal labor, and the military and business endeavors around the globe that have left US citizens in poverty—to the point that there will not be a taxbase left to fund this expansion by a certain time (we will say 2150 AD).

In the US, we attempt to be rational and prudent about our government expenditures, but many times, both political parties say that taxes are being used egregiously. As the author has made a point to say throughout this book, a meager reallocation of DOD funds would fund almost any initiative either party wants; but tax reallocation is not the matter in this chapter. What we see is an appeal to the people: the party politicians either say "they are over-taxing you and want to put the government's hands in everything" or "they are under-taxing the powerful and limiting government capabilities to be effective." They will never bring up other sources of funding or ways to make the tax code work because it is either difficult, complicated, boring, or they do not know.

All that matters to the politician is getting elected, and they will discuss "hot topics" to win your favor. All that matters to the people is supporting their party and feeling validated. Political theatre is something that we will return to shortly, but first we need to continue comparing our realities with Machiavelli's thoughts on government spending. As Machiavelli said: "A prince therefore, … ought not, if he is wise, mind having a reputation for stinginess: in time he will always come to be considered more generous, when it is seen that, through his parsimony, he can make do with the resources he has, … without weighing his people down with taxation" and, with regard to generosity of spoils of war, "spending what belongs to others does not ruin your reputation, but rather adds to it: it is only spending what is yours that harms you" (Machiavelli, 2009).

In the United States, we do well to "spend what belongs to others," but we do not have practical parsimony. We continue to use military force and intelligence agencies, and lax international laws, to allow for cheap products and "hot commodities" like crude oil to make it seem like the riches of the world are plunder to share. They come from sources which use unethical labor, child labor, forced labor, slavery, and human rights abuses—but it does not harm a politician at home. Some citizens take advantage of broken systems, from civil contracting to welfare, but they only fall through the cracks because the cracks exist—if you fix a system's flaws, it will operate better. Furthermore, the government mismanages taxes in many of these instances, and in our system, that is basically spending what is not theirs. It is supposed to be allocated by them but with the wishes and needs of the people in mind.

At home, representatives make sure it seems like the majority of taxes are being used up for something other than National Security and Defense. They get support based on demonizing the other political party, because "they have spent your taxes" or "they gave the rich tax-cuts." This is a symptom of a globalized diffusion of responsibility. On a personal level, the diffusion of responsibility works like this: you hear screaming from nearby apartments—oh, someone else will call the police. On a global-organizational level, it works as follows. The markets are down, blame another country; the prices are up, blame another country; there are no jobs, blame another country; the national debt continues to skyrocket, blame it on global markets; your taxes were raised, blame it on the other party; there are too many people unemployed or on welfare, blame it on the other party...and so on.

We split from what Machiavelli saw because we do not have government parsimony, even though some may maintain the illusion that we do. We cannot make do with the resources given because our infrastructure, education, healthcare systems, social services, and criminal justice do not have the funds they need to be successful. In the US, we do not have the top test scores, the highest quality of life, accessible healthcare for all, or a booming economy filled with well-paid jobs. There has been too much generosity to certain sectors of the government, and to empire-building and neo-colonization in foreign countries.

The people are full of contempt, but the media mirage, political non-answers, and group polarization have left people confused as to why they are angry. The people have been left behind in the US, with most of their troubles meaning nothing to those who refuse to look at the bigger picture and the responsibility of the government. Along with the diffusion of responsibility, because of global trends that oppress everyone within and without the US, the politician would say that it is up to the people to figure out their problems—

just vote for me. Everything is about competition, everything is Darwinian, and if you do not have the survival skills to adapt to the "New World Order," then you will suffer for your inability to conform. On a policy level, blame is hardly ever placed on globalizing/monopolizing corporations, excessive funding to the DOD, mismanaged funds to government bodies, bad trade deals, or even something like modern mechanization practices, which render workers obsolete.

Too much generosity, as Machiavelli would have it, would make the people angry because you would run out of funds, and then their reliance on you is shattered and they are angry. As well, too much generosity would have made monarchs and aristocrats tax the people to make up for losses, which breeds contempt. Over-taxation is not an American problem; however, the problem is a bad tax code and poorly allocated taxes. Government actors, from Congressional representatives to Presidential Cabinet members, do not like to change what works for them if it is bad for their donors, and they do not like to admit faults.

In the realm of American Exceptionalism, nothing ever seems to be our fault because "we are the greatest country on the planet" and "we have the best economy in the world" and, according to politicians, "without the military in its current form we would live in dystopia." If taxes were utilized rationally, and to the benefit of the people, there could be systematic generosity without over-taxation. Generosity is seen in how taxes are used, but they are used to further an agenda rather than true prosperity. Contrariwise, parsimony is not an American quality: we are a society of prodigious overconsumption and financial frivolity. In our political system, one party promises tax cuts, and the other promises socialized healthcare and education; either way, what we have is generosity-based electioneering.

The point remains to be said that so many people are disillusioned with politics and do not think their voice matters, that we have a third of a nation who does not vote or believe in the US government. The leaders have followed through on the most basic of matters: ensuring trade, taking a census, apportioning tax funds to infrastructure, education, and welfare systems (Medicaid/Medicare, food stamps, social security, unemployment), and setting the general standards for law and order. This means that leaders have followed through on meeting the basic needs of the people based on judicious use of tax funds and the ability to create laws. But many of these systems are failing due to a crumbling infrastructure with no guidance, budget cuts with more demands, and a gross misappropriation of funds. There are auditing agencies which have surely made the same arguments.

The military obviously gets the largest portion of tax funds annually. So, is that where our priorities lie? Has the approach of "offense as defense" become more important in foreign lands instead of using that initiative to ensure a prosperous populace? Machiavelli knew that defense was important, because if you could not defend your kingdom, then you were weak; but what also makes a Prince weak is his inability to prudently see to the needs of his people. To Machiavelli, this is because he will be despised and hated and eventually deposed or assassinated. When we have one in eight Americans living below the poverty line, it is time for the shepherd to stop and look at his flock, and, as Machiavelli would say, "keep his word."

Since an allusion to the Romans has been made throughout this book, the lesson that can be learned from them in this chapter is this: as soon as they expanded too far, and forgot about their motherland, the Roman Empire disintegrated from over-taxation of the poor, corruption, famine, disease, uprisings, and invasions. If the Empire had focused its attention on manageable properties, and its own citizens, they may have prospered for much longer than they did. However, when your agenda exceeds your capabilities, you are doomed to fail on that front and in the eyes of your citizens. The mission becomes unsustainable. It is the geopolitical equivalent of your "eyes being bigger than your stomach."

Machiavelli very often refers to the failings of the Roman Empire, Kings of the late Medieval period and Renaissance, and contemporary Princes in Italy, and the stories end with the royalty and aristocrats attempting to dominate everything and losing their lives. The concept of an ever-expanding Empire is not possible because eventually the people will be paying for actions around the world, with not much money or protection in their homeland—this is a recipe for chaos. With too much hubris and greed, the obsession of acquiring land, power, and possessions will be an exercise in futility. The futility comes from the fact that expansionism will eventually neither protect you nor make you wealthy. It ends in the decline of an Empire, which could be averted. The Roman, Chinese, Persian, Holy Roman, and Saracen Empires lasted long enough to have Golden Ages in which they did not expand too far, or it did not cost extra to expand, and they had wise rulers who understood the obligations of a ruler to its people: maintain the state and keep your people prosperous.

Politicians have the power to change some of the issues that have been mentioned throughout this text, and the people have to advocate for real changes to be made on a global scale. The US acts like its problems are worse than anywhere else and that our problems are all domestic; they are not. Politicians will always promise things they will not achieve, and they will fail to please everyone. It is not an easy job. But their ability to achieve goals on a policy level is the only way we start to see change. Many philosophies around the world believe that change starts from within, and in the case of the US empire, that is also true. Politicians need to be courageous and stand up for the American people while also showing the nations of the Earth respect for their own sovereignty. For many politicians, the problem is that they are careerists: they are only worried about reelection instead of the issues. One must focus on pleasing what the masses think is a perfect system so they can avoid being voted out of office. The masses will not always understand why certain policy changes must be made, or the complexities behind an issue, but then the politician should educate them. Instead of that, they usually revert to party politics, policies that are "business as usual," and focusing on reelection.

Machiavelli realized that many elements of geopolitics are a show, hence the term "political theatre." But he always saw all of the necessary qualities of rulers, which could be described as a cult of personality, to be tools in a toolbox. They are meant to be used, when applicable, to either maintain power or please the people. Machiavelli made this clear when he made this statement in *The Prince*:

> A prince … must seem, in what he says and how he looks, to be full of mercy, full of faith, full of integrity, full of humanity, full of religion… Everyone can see who you seem to be, few can sense who you are; and those few do not dare to oppose the opinion of so many who have the majesty of the state to defend them; … A prince should therefore act in such a way as to maintain the state: the means will always be judged honorable and praised by everybody, because the common people are always taken by appearances and results; and in the world there is nothing but the common people, and there is no room for the few while the many have something to lean on (Machiavelli, 2009).

And we see that in the US every election cycle. The candidates have to show their family, their career experience, and especially make it clear that they are Christian. This also ties back to Max Weber, because people vote based on religion because they believe that the matters of this nation are ordained by God. Without someone Christian, they believe, the nation will fall into ruin. When in reality, the only nation that was under the protection of God, according to the Bible, was Judea; and it is not clear if that still remains. Now, none of that matters when it comes to the ability to govern or make great policies, but it matters to the emotions of the voters. Machiavelli knew that well when he said that rulers must *seem* to be full of integrity, humanity, and religion. The people voting want to know that the person who governs them, or is their representative, is like them; and it does not matter if they really are. And the politician must always act as if they understand the struggle of their base, when, in reality, they rarely do.

What would be recommended, to make substantive change from policy, is use Machiavellian tactics wisely. No one can deny that they are used in politics. The point of Machiavellianism is winning your prize, and the end always justifies the means. So, if there is something that must be done on specific policies which do not make it into the press conferences, debates, and various TV appearances, then choose what works best in the moment: keep them hidden until it is a great time to promote a certain Bill, or make them public if the world will push for its enactment. Keep intentions of policies secret, as others are taught to do, until it is the right time to bring it to the floor or the court of public opinion.

Every political candidate puts on this show of how they will "work for you" or "bring your voice" to the political arena. Congressional members should make their foci: 1) reallocation of funds from the DOD to other sectors of government *regardless* of protests about patriotism and stopping the "enemy," and 2) trust-busting, anti-lobbyism, and forcing production in the US *regardless* of what US companies which have globalized say. That would be a political show to which even Machiavelli himself would give kudos. The people may be outraged, but if they are properly educated on the matters at hand, then they will know the reasons for the moves—and they will support what is best for their nation, at least.

Even Machiavelli himself was making a plea to the princes in his time to unify the land, maintain noble governance, and stop the endless wars, skirmishes, invasions, and alliances which were ruining the quality of life for Renaissance Italians. Machiavelli was a cynical nationalist who wanted to convince the Medici, and others from the ruling classes, to unite and fight against foreign influences and power. He wanted his country to be brought out of divisions that were ripping apart the fabric of Italian society. Machiavelli has been given a bad reputation, but, in reality, Machiavelli was raised in a country that was experiencing colonialism, sectarianism, assassinations, warfare, and corruption, and *The Prince* is "an exhortation to take Italy out of the hands of the barbarians and liberate her" (Machiavelli, 2009). Machiavelli endorsed the idea of "fighting fire with fire" in the sociopolitical context he was in. Machiavelli's country was much more of a victim of colonialism rather than a colonial empire. The last time Italy was ever an empire was during the time of the Romans. And, as it turns out, it seems as if Machiavelli would be opposed to many kinds of imperialism, especially if it meant jeopardizing the unity and functionality of the state.

The Rules of the Game of Power

The US, and plenty of nations, conform to Machiavellian criteria. In reality, one just has to look back throughout time, and at one point, there will be a massive expanding empire in a region that you literally handpick on a globe. These rules of power that were adopted as part of this book's pretext are the "playbook" that empires throughout all time have used. These rules, and others, and the violation of all, have been part of the formula which is known to topple opponents. As a closing analysis, a small foray into the Rules of the Game of Power will allow for skepticism towards the rules themselves, and if there are useful additions to be made when comparing them to Machiavelli's *The Prince*. So, with consideration of the examples used in case studies, policy discussions, and philosophizing, we shall see if the rules can be *bona fide*.

> <u>*Rule #1*</u>: *Have the hard power (military/police) and soft power (cultural influence and laws) to own land, tax the people, and generate immense amounts of work and trade.*

This notion of neo-colonization always has a military element to it: Japan and Germany were both subjected to American control for reasons ranging from restitution for WWII or retaliation for events that transpired in WWII. Germany began to pay us, and into the international system, and Japan became a fully occupied territory. The Korean War was a success on both fronts of protecting people from Communism and occupying. After the Korean War, except for Vietnam, covert operations were used to expand influence and "defeat" Communism until the Gulf War. Chile, Congo, Cuba, Egypt, Iraq, Israel, Nicaragua, and other nations have all had the CIA actively operating in their countries since the late 1950s until the 1990s.

Now, having hard power is easy, and having soft power is a little trickier but very manageable. However, in the modern context, you cannot tax everyone as a nation. In this first Rule, it states that the Game of Power is to "own land, tax the people, and generate immense amounts of wealth and trade." From a Machiavellian point of view, if you were not colonizing properly, you would lose your conquest. But Machiavelli would clearly want to delineate between powerful business alliances and occupation; however, some of the economic complexities and power structures of the modern day were not foreseeable to someone like Machiavelli. From a Machiavellian standpoint, if a merchant was not paying taxes to his nation, then he was failing his civic duties. Because how can a prince operate with no taxes in an age of coin?

In the US, corporations definitely avoid due taxes when they have operations overseas, but the Treasury and the White House like the sales-tax that rolls in when they bring all of their goods. However, as an Empire, we are not able to tax all of the areas where the US has a massive influence. Globalization may have harmed the world with regard to unethical labor and climate change, but its system forces common people to need the jobs in their area; they cannot avoid it. Enough money will be generated via transactions, transnational business, shipping, and travel to allow losses in outright taxes. Which means a lot of spending and selling, creating sales tax but not any domestic jobs.

> _Rule #2_: _Use international trade and influence to have at least soft power over the lands which you do not have hard power over._

This closes the gap from the last Rule because, with modern Empire, you cannot always have hard power in every place where you have authority. Naturally, this is due to international alliances and law, and because of the logistical nightmare that it would be to use Roman tactics to infiltrate the world in the ways that have been accomplished since WWII. Soft power is necessary to extend your sphere of influence in such a ubiquitous and subliminal fashion that everyone wants to be like the "Leaders of the Free World," and they do not always know why. The second rule has been just as useful as the first.

This is because messaging can be very important top-down, from government documents to the masses, with regard to ideologies, philosophies, fears, and ideals. Mass media reports and angles, which affect support given to politicians, reflect certain messages about the status quo. Spokespeople in international alliances can voice disapproval to the actions of other nations or call for summits of international governance organizations. If you have soft power in a multitude of countries, then you control the message. The message is, it is "us" versus "them," "Neoliberalism" versus "Communism"—and they must not win. American media, clothes, technologies, political movements, history, international law, trade deals, and cultural impressions on so many nations is an overarching example of how the Imperial-Industrial Complex has succeeded in having its products and messages in every place which will buy, or sell, its story.

> *Rule #3: Utilize the power of "the power of the people," which entices citizens to be a part of the large matrix of the "Imperial-Industrial Complex"—in every country in which you have hard and soft power.*

The people are a part of this large narrative of ending communism and upholding the "civilized" world. They are a part of it through upbringing and the beliefs that are taught to them by school, their community, their nation, and, generally, the whole of society. Here are some elements of "power of the people" which are used to indoctrinate the populace to serve without question: "strive for the American dream"; "support the troops and stand for the flag"; "spend your money as often as you can to be a contributor to the economy"; "buying materials will give you status and happiness"; "live to work" (instead of working to live); "enemies are trying to destroy the US and her allies every day"; "monopolies are great innovations"; "the stock market is an indicator of economic prosperity"; and, in the US, "everything the US does is right." Dissenting against these ideas is usually met with repercussions in a disciplinary fashion, or judgment and ostracization via the "court of public opinion."

Some of the notions embedded into the "American Mindset" are not awful, such as work ethic, supporting Constitutional rights, and patriotism for justified military action, but the ironic part is that typical "American Values" are omitted from the Imperial-Industrial Complex. Constitutional rights are violated at home, funds are mismanaged by the government, and "Life, Liberty, and the Pursuit of Happiness" are difficult in the Age of Waxing and Waning Depressions, which is based on global successes. Around the world, freedoms are violated, human rights are abused, and it turns out that the United States in the role of several nations' "Big Brother" turns us into a bully who does not care much about peacekeeping. All of this in order to fuel the state-corporate conquest of the world and its resources while simultaneously ensuring that the Communists never get their paws on these lands and goods.

The power of the people is useful because they will support what is "best" for their nation every time. What is typically "the best" is sounding powerful, and sounding like you will get some results—but to the trained ear, the words of politicians sound like non-answers and rhetoric. What is best in the political arena is "being tough on China," even though they ironically own our debt and we will never be too tough on them; "being tough on Russia," even though they get away scot-free with crimes and will always be excellent trading partners with Europe—our allies that need Russian resources; and "creating jobs, managing taxes and healthcare, and instilling law and order" are the goals in the US. Recently, there has been discussion about taxing the wealthiest one percent of society. These taxes will not save us, although it may be a worthwhile tax-code alteration.

You will not hear many politicians say that all federal tax dollars need to be evaluated based on extant evidence of need, and then appropriated as such. This should happen as pragmatic governance, and the extra funding should come from where there is a surplus and/or waste. We will not hear many politicians blame banking laws, international business laws, and corporate trends for our domestic financial issues. We will not hear them support laws to change them. There will only be calls to take away money from the CEOs, who, from so many people's perspectives, are clearly the only people to blame. People like to put a face to a problem, but when problems are systemic, so are the solutions.

As we have covered, fear is used in this day and age to keep people obedient to the whims of the Imperial-Industrial Complex. This is similar to what was seen in bygone eras, but in this day and age, it has morphed to become a manipulation rather than a disciplinary example. In the past, if someone defied the wishes of their ruler, they would very likely be hanged or decapitated as a traitor, or for various other concocted reasons (heresy, witchcraft, and treason for example). This would serve as an example to the commonwealth of their duty to obey. In modernity, fear is utilized by many leaders as a sociopolitical tool rather than a cautionary tale. Fear of the enemy, fear of unwanted policies, fear of a foreign threat, fear of unemployment, and fear of change are all used to galvanize the people to work harder, support an agenda, and hate all things which disrupt the status quo. So, from kindergarten to adulthood, there are many ways that governments ensure that we are willing, and uninformed, participants in the Imperial-Industrial Complex—and if you oppose it, then you are a "sympathizer" of "unpatriotic" ideals.

> _Rule #4_: _Create regulatory bodies (regulatory agencies, courts, councils for treaties) and force everyone to follow the same rules of engagement._

A few things that all empires throughout time have done is establish their own colonies, governors, courts, tax codes, and trade routes. Modern empires have differed from ancient empires in many ways, from the way they colonize to the ways in which people support it with resources, and the same is true with the types of regulatory bodies which are created for an international body politic. The regulatory bodies in the United States can be the SEC, FCC, FDA, EPA, and a variety of courts and credentialing organizations. The only people who are exempt from the laws and regulations, which are imposed on everyday citizens, are those in government and corporations which can pay the fines or avoid punishment legally. That is also true internationally.

The international regulatory bodies, including but not limited to the United Nations, the World Trade Organization, the International Criminal Court, and the North Atlantic Treaty Organization, attempt to ensure that all signatory parties abide by the same rules outlined in treaties and agreements. The World Trade Organization does not allow bans on lead, hormones, unethical harvesting/slaughter of animals, child labor, underpaid labor, unsafe mining/working conditions, materials lacking exact provenance, or anything that could cause a hardship on the country which is trading a product which was either produced in an inhumane fashion or can cause health problems. It is said that bans which come from one country will create a ripple effect that will ruin free trade for many nations. This "no ban" policy has even thwarted bans the US attempted to put into place, but generally, the World Trade Organization works in favor of the Imperial-Industrial Complex.

The United Nations and NATO are historically on the side of the United States. The United Nations cannot defy the wishes of the United States because the United States is the main "shareholder" in the international governing body. The UN often does the bidding of the US agenda with trade embargos and getting so many nations to comply with International Humanitarian and Human Rights laws—except the five veto powers of the UN (US, UK, Russia, China, France). These five veto powers of the UN have the ability to ignore the UN with no consequences. Subsequently, efforts which combine the Imperial-Industrial Complex with the mission of the UN have been very profitable and necessarily invasive. These would be the operations of the International Monetary Fund and the World Bank.

Along with ignoring international law, as has been stated many times in this text, the US has not ratified the Rome Statute and will never have any of its politicians being tried for breaching sections of the Geneva Conventions. The US will not prosecute their own corporations or government officials for violations of International Humanitarian/Human Rights laws regardless of ratification status. This has been proven historically and categorically, allowing the US to pursue its agenda with little-to-no interference. Regulatory bodies serve to create laws and standards for most countries, and for the common person, but to a nation that sees itself as the "Peacekeeper of the World," there is no place for anyone else's ideologies or laws. There is only maintaining the sovereign status of the US, the machine of international business, and the illusion that we abide by all international laws.

Rule #5: _Capitalize and Avoid Taxation, Fines, and Prosecution_

Obviously. And this point has been belabored throughout this book. The damaging effects of the elite searching for resources and wealth, based on globalizing their power, have been seen in many populations of the world. Average citizens, in many countries, are bound to the systems created by a global superpower. It is in that way that many peoples across the Earth are similar, among so many other ways that we all share a common bond. Certain elements of globalization are perfect for our modern lives. Other elements, like those of expansionism, illegal action, corruption, and calculated indifference towards the plight of the poor, will be the undoing of the very foundations that this Empire has struggled to build. The US Imperial-Industrial Complex has already stretched out too far, and it is that problem which will be the focus of discussion for the rest of this book.

Chapter 8:

Armistice, Populism, and The Humble Bows of Sovereign Nations

"In a country well governed, poverty is something to be ashamed of.
In a country badly governed, wealth is something to be ashamed of."
~ Confucius in the 'Analects'

A few things that could be used in modern geopolitical solutions are harmony, diplomacy, and mutual respect for sovereign nations' decisions that are made for the good of their national population. The last item on that list has been called nationalism, protectionism, and some call it populism. Populism is the best phrase to use for the purposes of this text, because it does not have a negative stigma like the other terms. In a democratic nation, populism will mean tending to the needs of the majority of citizens before the needs of a few elite. The few elite refers to the federal government (and its various extensions), the economic regulators of international trade, and the corporate executives who are involved in globalizing their workforce. If policies and laws were passed on foreign and domestic levels, by the US regarding China and vice versa, for example, these two countries could learn to serve their own people and work together. This will happen by collaboration, intentional international summits, and conventions on trade, and pure will, to make healthier and happier working people. Fittingly, the partnership of the US and China should look like the "Yin and Yang" symbol. In the context of the UN and the WTO, these countries could have a lot of sway in rearranging what international trade and utilitarian populism look like from North and South America to Eurasia and Africa.

For the United States, a self-aware assessment of the domestic production needs and poverty rates will need to be administered to determine how to elevate the quality of life for American citizens by economic and trade policies. The US also needs to convene practical meetings with nations about deals like NAFTA, TPP, and the Uruguay Round Agreements, just to name a few transnational trade deals. These discussions should ascertain what is best for Mexico, Canada, China, Japan, Korea, Spain, Greece, Vietnam, India, and so many other nations, and practical laws should be enacted to come to the best solutions which help the most people based on a plethora of needs and risk factors. What would also be nice is the eventual agreement to ratify and abide by international law, across the board, and at least be striving for that goal if not fully achieving it. Obviously, this would all take years, and sounds very utopian, but it is all quite possible.

New regulations could easily be added to the WTO or the Organization for Economic Cooperation and Development (OECD) by Agreement or Treaty. Through G20 Summits, UN Conventions, international treaties, and trade meetings, there could be many new developments which affect every country's role in international trade. These role changes could be made part of an overall agenda which promotes business trends that help the citizens of a sovereign nation and promote international trade rather than trends which just promote trade but do not benefit corporations' homelands. The Americas, China, Russia, Africa, and the EU need to look at one another, face to face, and negotiate trade deals and laws which protect their people's quality of life and maintain international trade.

This would mean deglobalizing certain corporations and economies while, perhaps, sending international production to countries that need more stimulation. Bolstering domestic production will lead to trade deals which play on countries' strong exports in an international market, while importing goods a society does not abundantly produce. But the hope would be that imported goods and exported goods reach an international equilibrium on what is needed. Relationships for mutual benefit are great, but they should not just benefit the few elites in government and business. To love others, you must love yourself first—and so it goes with nations. Focusing on what makes a nation great, from its people, to its culture, to its unique commodities, can help make a nation a great global partner as well. Domestic production, international standards of safety and health in the workplace, compliance with international business laws and treaties, and a focus on limiting human rights abuses and economic injustices will all be the hallmarks to indicate the start of a new chapter, which is introspective, then circumspect. The belief systems of the East and the West would agree on measures that facilitate harmony, balance, and stability as they relate to alliances and partnerships.

Along those lines, the US and Russia must confront the realities of the modern era, which is like an extension of the Cold War. These governments must find solutions to the trade problems and negotiate a treaty regarding the paramilitary problems. The call to action the author would make is that the US and Russia should agree on a UN Convention resulting in a treaty. This treaty could address the actions of both countries in foreign lands, decide who the definitive superpower is in a given area, and command a ceasefire and armistice in all areas where military or intelligence operations are active. As well, these countries could limit overt and covert missions by agreeing to operate based on nations asking for assistance. And perhaps this is too much to ask for, but what is needed is new alliances. What is also needed is a shift in governance, where the needs of those oppressed by current structures are assisted with policy change. For it is the charge of the government to maintain order, and to ensure a prosperous citizenry.

The East and the West share common ideologies which have been deviated from. As Jesus said to his disciples in Luke 6:31, "Do unto others as you would have them do unto you," which has been coined the "Golden Rule" in popular parlance. Some say "Treat others as you wish to be treated," but the point remains that nations need diplomacy, and regular folks need civility. In conjunction with the teachings of helping the poor in the Bible, the "Golden Rule" will also encompass empathy and sympathy: you may not be in the situation they are in, but if you can help, then you should, because it is probably how you would wish to be treated. Confucius also stated something very similar to what Christ had to offer when he said, "Do not impose on others what you yourself would not desire." The theme ranges from humane treatment on a personal level to the idea that helping the weak will make society strong. Confucius was wise when he stated this chapter's quote, as it directly relates to mismanagement of governance and how it is reflected in the quality of life of the citizenry. When your nation is struggling, the focus should be on the nation so that you can live up to your expectations. If there are problems that must be addressed, they cannot go to the wayside or the backburner if they directly affect your population.

As stated before, these ideologies have been deviated from. The Communism that occurred in Stalin's Gulags or Mao's Great Leap Forward is a Communism that deviated from the idea of everyone being equal. Because everyone was equal—except that those who found themselves in power were far superior. This power was a Stanford Prison Experiment on the most grotesque levels—just as WWII was genocide and warfare in its worst forms. Because of the aftermath of arguably the most traumatic years in the planet's history, every country took drastic measures that varied by locale.

We have discussed what some of those drastic measures have looked like in the US, and with its international interests. After all, drastic times call for drastic measures. However, that time is past. We should not be in a new Cold War. We should not still be an occupying force in over eighty countries and in control of the world's top regulators from the UN to the WTO to NATO. The main reason is because, with our military, intelligence, and business interests in foreign lands, the US has abandoned its people in a depressive civilization which is the most inhumane of all developed nations. The efforts of globalized greed have resulted in more than cheap labor and stolen resources, but what also has been stolen is something that is not tangible to the governments or businesses: careers in the US. The secondary reason why we should not be the "Global Police," nor an American Empire, is because we should be focusing on diplomacy and collaboration while simultaneously moving forward from a Cold War framework.

Defeating Communism seems to cost a lot of money, and Communism does not seem to be going anywhere. And in fact, we have a good relationship with China that needs to be even better regulated and mediated. Russia is another story entirely, especially with regard to all of the secrecy about their KGB operations, the assassinations of spies or political detractors who defect, and the on-and-off skirmishes with the Marines or Navy SEALs in nations where alliances and rulers are not firmly established. Yet Germany was a devastatingly destructive force during WWII, towards any and all who would defy the Reich, and the Russians lost many more soldiers in that fight than the US did. They were an ally then. The US lost hundreds of thousands of men to Germany and her allies, and at this moment, the US has a great relationship with Germany. There are US military bases in Germany, and the Germans are still paying reparations for WWII, and that surely sets the tone of the alliance. Nonetheless, they are now an ally, and arrangements have been made between so many nations that were enemies in the past. Russia does a lot of business with the European Union, just as we do. Just as we do with Japan. The point is, we are talking about two superpower UN members who have the ability to change the dynamics of geopolitics if they were so inclined. Nobody thinks the US or Russia will stop their program of global espionage, or seeking influence, but treaties and trade deals which include the topics of highly specific disarmaments, trade partners, and privileges of sovereignty in a modern international community would make an excellent foundation for future progress.

China and Mexico need to be brought up in this context as well. Those two countries are intertwined into the US's GDP in a way that makes one imagine the strands of a rope coiling to become one. Mexicans labor tirelessly to give the US a large amount of produce and merchandise. As of July 1st, 2020, the new NAFTA is the USMCA, or United States-Mexico-Canada Agreement, and the United States should continue to work with these countries to find an equilibrium of jobs in the US, Mexico, and Canada that benefits all parties. What the US truly needs is more production in the US, and allowing the Visa and "Guest Worker" programs with Mexico to work more smoothly as they did in the past. This would also mean demilitarizing the border to an extent—and could eventually lead to talks which make the immigration process efficient. Without the new "wall" that was built, the US-Mexico border was already the most militarized border of two nations at peace.

With more immigration, and more production in the US, we would see an economic "win-win" situation. Many people are scared of immigrants from Mexico because of what they hear about cartels, but there is no correlation between immigration and an increase in violent crime (Flagg, 2019). As well, the only reason why groups like the Sinaloa Cartel, formerly led by El Chapo, and Colombian cocaine dealers like Pablo Escobar's are so successful is because the US is their main customer. The Sinaloa Cartel makes a majority of their profits from selling marijuana, which is becoming more accepted and legalized in the US, and with legalization, we would see a decrease in the prominence of the Sinaloa Cartel. However, members of cartels are not the people seeking asylum or a new home; Sinaloa Cartel members thrive in their homeland. It is others who do not. As well, there are many people crossing the border for a variety of reasons, and it does not have to do with drug lords or infiltrating the US. The other insinuation leveled at immigrants is that they are "human trafficking." This term has been very misleading in nearly all forms of its circulation. The majority of human trafficking in the world is labor trafficking. The US profits from many forms of labor trafficking around the world—these are people who are made to work without their consent, either child, underpaid, or slave labor, and they can be relocated to a new area or work in their region of residence. Sex trafficking very often happens within family groups, and the victims need only be exploited, not transported. This is why the Preventing Sex Trafficking and Strengthening Families Act of 2014 was passed (NCSL, 2016). As well, the US does not have statistics on sex trafficking but makes wild assumptions, while the UN has stated that seven out of ten sex trafficking victims are from Asia (Kelly, 2019). So, we really need to reevaluate our priorities, and our relationship with our brethren to the south; we are, after all, the Americas.

"The Future Global Order Will Be Managed by the US and China – Get Used to It" is the title of an article from the World Economic Forum, and it succinctly states my purpose in discussing US-China relations (Muggah and Tiberghien, 2018). No matter what, China is a pioneer in infrastructure development, carbon neutral initiatives, urbanization, class elevation, and new sophistications in science, technology, and education. China has recently built the longest road known to man, and the longest bridge, which connects mainland China to Hong Kong. They have, in a rogue fashion, tested gene-editing to extents that western scientists have not attempted. Furthermore, they have created a generator that can reach the temperature of the sun, putting them ever closer to fusion energy and various advances in energy and science. As well, they have become a society of hyper-surveillance in their urban areas, just as many western cities have done, such as London, England, or New York City. They have done well for their people, and even though they have a long way to go to become a transparent and liberally free society, they are our partners. We should work together as partners and attempt to bury the hatchet on old qualms. China needs to adhere to international laws, just as the US does, and once again, we are talking about superpowers who can arrange Summits and Conventions for their own purposes. To reiterate, the US, the UK, France, China, and Russia are the most powerful UN members.

The first order of business should be to have more production in the US, and do not make it seem like China or Mexico "stole our jobs." Corporations have been offshoring because of the large profit margins they receive for a long time. China can still have staple factories and businesses that are from the US, surely, but anything that can be removed and replaced with another country's companies, including China's, would be excellent for the US. However, China does own a majority of our national debt in Treasury bonds, and they benefit from our business relationship, but some strong terms are going to need negotiating to pay off that debt and increase the quality of life for workers in the US and China. The second order of business will need to be trading standards, which rely on the strengths of the continent(s) in question. If an item can be produced in North or South America, then the Americas should trade within their continents. If there is a need for international trade, then execute transportation of goods (like soybeans to China, or factory-made goods sent from China to the Americas). Generally, Asia and the EU could work on continent-reliant strategies as well. Trading mainly locally, with international trade being about what nations cannot produce, has been the nature of trade for many centuries.

Conclusion

The nations of the world need to get back to their foundational roots of peaceful ideologies. This means civility, diplomacy, and working towards the common good. It also means strengthening our own societies instead of focusing on offshoring and global trade while putting profit margins over an able-bodied citizen workforce. And do not mistake this semi-utopian rhetoric to mean that all societies have been peaceful, but rather that the peoples of the world almost all have prophets and philosophers who set the tone for wise governance in antiquity. Usually, texts like the Bible, or the Analects of Confucius, were the foundations for laws in the East and West. This is also not a proposal to create theocratic states, but to simply be aware of the good that can be accomplished with competent and service-oriented governments. Legal scholars of the West, such as John Locke, John Stuart Mill, Alexander Hamilton, and so many others, posited that laws should be for the benefit of the people—just as their many inspirations wrote.

We must not have different empires vying for power and control on a global scale. The expansion, and crippling, of empires has been well documented throughout time; it is a conquest of futility. The goal of conquering the world almost always leaves the homeland in one kind of turmoil, and, in nations which get conquered (or occupied), the turmoil is of a different kind. However, if the empires agree to limit expansion, negotiate trade deals and territories effectively, and resolve Cold War issues of how societies are governed (neoliberal capitalism versus modern communism), and espionage and nuclear arsenals, then these titans of industry and global preeminence can cohabitate on this planet more effectively. And when certain countries try to impose standards on another that they will not accept, then sometimes we have to accept defeat. Or, more precisely, we would see many compromises during negotiations as grand as have been proposed in this chapter.

In the US specifically, we need transparency in politics. Politicians continue these never-ending cycles, and then try to find blame and solutions in a system which they, the military budget which they approve, and corporations have created. Transparency in this scenario means being honest about US failures with tax management and international business policies and treaties. And from that benchmark of admitting what the problems are, the US can continue to progress; as they say, the first step is admitting you have a problem. However, the US has envisioned itself as the "Peacekeeper," the "Leader of the Free World" and as exceptionally sovereign. This is seen in its blind ambition, disregard for consequences, and inability to make policy changes which upset the "New World Order." For example, it is easier to continue trade in the network which is already established instead of updating laws and standards based on needs of human rights, safety, and economic justice. As well, most politicians are afraid of criticizing the national security and defense sectors of the government, because they will potentially be heralded as unpatriotic. If all parties were honest about what is needed, and explained why a certain amount of money could be reallocated from the DOD to other sectors of government (Department of Education, Health & Human Services, Housing and Urban Development, Department of Labor), then people would start to understand. But, once again, this is about breaking myths about our country, and its role on a global scale, and about general transparency.

The rehabilitation of the United States can be achieved, for the populace that seems to struggle with unemployment, depression, addiction, and trauma, and for those in government who can truly feel like they support the American Dream. The American Dream in its current state is akin to an American Scheme: the country where all the children in the first grade are told they can be president, and by the eleventh grade, their teachers have told them to get used to flipping burgers. Where it is said that you can achieve your dreams, but that will depend on if you can afford college, if there are jobs available, and if you have the necessary supports. Where you are made to believe that you must be married, own a house and car, and spend your money on the endless conveyor belt of mass consumption, only to find that to go into debt to be an adult is a myth. Where old racial policies on drugs, segregation, religion, and terrorism are not rectified in law, and the rhetoric encourages people to join polarized groups to continue cycles of bigotry and hatred. Where we think of ourselves as saviors of the world, but we are in fact an American Empire that demands alliances, legally or illegally.

Many people think that the US has a national religion, and it does not, but the main religion of the US is not of supernatural origin: the religion is capitalism. Capitalism and democracy are great systems, but we have worshipped them to the point of being blind, and not challenging our faith. To the point that we have one in eight American families living in poverty in "the greatest nation on the planet," while others make dividends on deals happening half a world away. And guess what. The citizenry did not get a vote on the laws and deals which affect their livelihood. The elite have come to only care about power over their subjects, and making money, to achieve a status of giant among the ants, regardless of what happens to the ants. We have taught ourselves that nothing is our fault, and correspondingly, no one takes responsibility from the highest offices in the land to your average civilian. The devil is in the details, and it is time to take action against the devil. The devil, this time, being our sour spirit of capitalism that is trying to possess the world with its promises. To the lawmaker who may read this text, take into account the policy recommendations which have been made, please. To the "average Joe or Jane" who happens to read this book, take the messages and policy recommendations and add them to your petitions, protests, questions, and movements for change in the United States.

Bibliography

(By chapter, in alphabetical order)

Chapter 1:

Ohio State University. The Northern Securities Case. Department of History. Website. https://ehistory.osu.edu/exhibitions/1912/trusts/NorthernSecurities

Chapter 2:

Asia-Pacific Economics Blog. Japan Suicide Statistics." Website. http://apec-sec.org/japan-suicide-statistics/

BBC. (2003). Congo: White King, Red Rubber, Black Death. Documentary. Website. https://www.youtube.com/watch?v=dAHxRD8dZOM

BBC. (2015). Democratic Republic of Congo profile-Timeline. Web. http://www.bbc.com/news/world-africa-13286306

Chambers, Andrew. (2010). Japan: ending the culture of the 'honourable' suicide. The Guardian. Web. http://www.theguardian.com/commentis-free/2010/aug/03/japan-honourable-suicide-rate

Dziesinski, Michael. (2004). Hikikomori: Investigations into the phenomenon of acute social withdrawal in contemporary Japan. University of Hawaii Manoa. Web. http://towakudai.blogs.com/Hikikomori.Research.Survey.pdf

Everyculture.com. "Japan". Website. http://www.everyculture.com/Ja-Ma/Japan.html

Funabachi, Yoichi. (1992). Japan and America: Global Partners. Foreign Policy, No. 86. Spring, pp. 24-39. Washington Post-Newsweek Interactive, LLC. Web. JSTOR.

IMF. (2020). The IMF and the World Bank. International Monetary Fund. Website. imf.org/en/About/Factsheets/Sheets/2016/07/27/15/31/IMF-World-Bank

Klein, Naomi. (2008). The Shock Doctrine: The Rise of Disaster Capitalism. Picador. Print.

Macmillan, Margaret. (2009). Rebuilding the world after the second world war. The Guardian. Website.
https://www.theguardian.com/world/2009/sep/11/second-world-war-rebuilding

McCurry, Justin. "Japan vows to cut suicide rate by 20% over 10 years." The Guardian. 2014. Web. Accessed 04/05/2015.
http://www.theguardian.com/world/2014/sep/04/japan-vows-suicide-rate-cut-cultural-resistance-mental-health

OHCHR. (2020). International Human Rights Law. United Nations Office of the High Commissioner on Human Rights. Website.

Rothe, Dawn L. (2009). State Criminality: The Crime of All Crimes. Lexington Books. Lanham, Maryland. Print.

Slater, Alice. (2018). The US has military bases in 80 countries. All of them must close. Pressenza. Website. pressenza.com/2018/02/us-military-bases-80-countries-must-close/

University of Minnesota. (2015). Ratification of International Human Rights Treaties – USA. Human Rights Library. Website. hrlibrary.umn.edu/research/ratification-USA.html

Chapter 3:

Brummer, Stefaans, Craig McKune and James Wood. (2012). Tokyo Sexwale and the DRC's Mr Grab [sic]. Mail & Guardian. Johannesburg, South Africa. Web. http://mg.co.za/article/2012-08-17-00-tokyo-sexwale-and-the-drcs-mr-grab

Dobbs, Michael. (2002). US Had Key Role in Iraq Buildup. Washington Post. Global Policy Forum. Website.
https://archive.globalpolicy.org/security/issues/iraq/saddam/2002/1230buildup.htm

Editors. (2020). Iran-Contra Affair. History Channel. Website.
https://www.history.com/topics/1980s/iran-contra-affair

Exoo, Calvin F. (2010). The Pen and the Sword. Sage Publications. Ch. 1,

Pg. 35. Website. www.sagepub.com/sites/default/files/upm-binaries/31944_1.pdf (Exoo, 2010) The Pen and the Sword

Free the Slaves. (2011). The Congo Report: Slavery in Conflict Minerals. Free the Slaves. Web. https://www.freetheslaves.net/wp-content/uploads/2015/03/The-Congo-Report-English.pdf

Global Witness. (2015). Digging for Transparency. Global Witness. London, UK. Web. https://www.globalwitness.org/en/campaigns/conflict-minerals/digging-transparency/

Global Witness. (2014). Congo's Secret Sales. Global Witness. London, UK. Web. https://www.globalwitness.org/en/campaigns/oil-gas-and-mining/congo-secret-sales/

Ismi, Asad. (2014). The Congo Still Ravaged by U.S. Funded Conflict and Plunder. Global Research. Web. http://www.globalresearch.ca/the-congo-still-ravaged-by-u-s-funded-conflict-and-plunder/5375098

Kavoussi, Bonnie. (2017). Average Cost Of A Factory Worker In The U.S., Germany and China [Infographic]. Huffpost. Website. https://www.huffpost.com/entry/average-cost-factory-worker_n_1327413?guccounter=1&guce_referrer=aHR0cHM6Ly93d3cuYmluZy5jb20vc2VhcmNoP3E9YXZlcmFnZStwYXkrb2YrYStjaGluZXNlK3dvcmtlcitjitjb21wYXJlZCt0byt0aGUrdXMmZm9ybT1FREdVQ1QmcXM9UEYmY3ZpZD1lZmFhODEyZmNkOWY0NDE3OGJiNjI2OTgxZmQwMWM1MiZyZWZpZz03M2JmYTMzOGNiNjY0Yjg5ODViZjg5ZmZhOGU5MDJlZSZjYz1VUyZzZXRsYW5nPWVuLVVVT&guce_referrer_sig=AQAAABNzNWPcTmpGoxw6BDZLcgqPWCBCg0K1an0mclB9W2vWc_QkJgqWjwUFo_FAtnxpAO_4tsyaBes5y_EXW2py1L-UTwP0ZIKGGjq_tsar5JsawpIDwQRNnh6dszo88XnxEE_p1xkQhYwB8gfsvFgtb7MjD4mX-YecgxzRGaY8x9

Leader, Daniel. (2008). Business and Human Rights-Time to Hold Companies to Account. International Criminal Law Review 8, pp 447-462. Martinus Nijhoff Publishers. Print.

Morphonios, Jake. (2014). Shocking Details About CIA Asset Saddam Hussein. Nolan Chart. Website. https://www.nolanchart.com/shocking-details-cia-asset-saddam-hussein#comment-16110

Rothe, Dawn L. (2009). State Criminality: The Crime of All Crimes. Lexington Books. Lanham, Maryland. Print.

Rothe, Dawn L. and Christopher W. Mullins. (2008). Gold, diamonds and blood: International state-corporate crime in the Democratic Republic of the Congo. Contemporary Justice Review, Vol. 11, No. 2, pp. 81-99. Routledge. Print.

United Nations Human Rights Office of the High Commissioner (OHCHR). (2010). DRC: Mapping human rights violations 1993-2003. UN. Web. http://www.ohchr.org/EN/Countries/AfricaRegion/Pages/RDCProjet-Mapping.aspx

Wallach, Lori and Michelle Sforza. (1999). Whose Trade Organization? Public Citizen. Print.

Chapter 4:

Amadeo, Kimberly. (2020a). Unemployment Rate by Year Since 1929 Compared to Inflation and GDP. The Balance. Website. https://www.thebalance.com/unemployment-rate-by-year-3305506

Amadeo, Kimberly. (2020b). US Debt to China, How Much, Reasons Why, and What If China Sells. The Balance. Website. https://www.thebalance.com/u-s-debt-to-china-how-much-does-it-own-3306355

Amadeo, Kimberly. (2020c). Will the U.S. ever pay off its debt? The Balance. Website. https://www.thebalance.com/will-the-u-s-debt-ever-be-paid-off-3970473

Beltran et al. (2012). Foreign Holdings of U.S. Treasuries and U.S. Treasury Yields. Federal Reserve. Website.https://www.federalreserve.gov/econres/ifdp/foreign-holdings-of-us-treasuries-and-us-treasury-yields.htm

Fessler, Pam. U.S. Census Bureau Reports Poverty Rate Down, But Millions Still Poor. (2019). NPR. Website.https://www.npr.org/2019/09/10/759512938/u-s-census-bureau-reports-poverty-rate-down-but-millions-still-poor

Goffman, Erving. (1963). Stigma: Notes on the Management of Spoiled Identity. Touchstone. Print.

Hagedorn, John. (2008). A World of Gangs. University of Minnesota Press. Print.

Huffpost. (2013). CEO-to-Worker Pay Ratio Ballooned 1000 Percent Since 1950: Report. Huffpost. Website. https://www.huffpost.com/entry/ceo-to-worker-pay-ratio_n_3184623

Martin, Emmie. (2019). This chart shows how much money Americans have

in savings at every age. CNBC. Website.
https://www.cnbc.com/2019/03/11/how-much-money-americans-have-in-their-savings-accounts-at-every-age.html

Maruna, Shadd. (2000). Making Good. American Psychological Association. Print.

McKellar, Katie. (2019). Utah's homeless experiment. Deseret News. Website.https://www.deseret.com/utah/2019/12/1/20985696/utah-road-home-homeless-shelter-salt-lake

Office of the Under Secretary of Defense. (2019). National Defense Budget Estimates for FY 2020. Department of Defense. PDF. FY 2020 PB Green Book (defense.gov)

Scruggs, Gregory. (2019). Once a national model, Utah struggles with homelessness. Reuters. Website. https://www.reuters.com/article/us-usa-homelessness-housing-idUSKCN1P41EQ

Simon et al. (2018). Addressing Poverty and Mental Illness. Psychiatric Times. Website. https://www.psychiatrictimes.com/view/addressing-poverty-and-mental-illness (Simon et al, 2018)

Chapter 5:

Bagdikian, Ben H. (2004). The New Media Monopoly. Penguin-Random House. Print.

Beckett, Stefan and Olivia Gazis. (2020). Senate Intelligence Committee releases final report on 2016 Russian Interference. CBS News. Website. https://www.cbsnews.com/news/senate-report-russian-interference-2016-us-election/

Bureau of Labor Statistics. (2020). Union Members Summary. Website. https://www.bls.gov/news.release/union2.nr0.htm

De Blasio, Bill. (2019). Why American Workers Need to be Protected From Automation. Wired. Website. https://www.wired.com/story/why-american-workers-need-to-be-protected-from-automation/

Firozi, Paulina. (2017). Trump names another Goldman Sachs executive to senior administration role. The Hill. Website. https://thehill.com/homenews/administration/324027-trump-names-another-goldman-sachs-exec-to-senior-administration-role

Frank, Thomas. (2016). Listen, Liberal -or- What Ever Happened to the Party of the People? Picador. Print.

King, Ledyard. (2019). Andrew Wheeler who's been leading Trump's deregulatory charge, confirmed by Senate as EPA chief. USA Today. Website. https://www.usatoday.com/story/news/politics/2019/02/28/trumps-new-epa-chief-andrew-wheeler-who-replaced-scott-pruitt/3014406002/

Lau, Tim. (2019). Citizens United Explained. Brennan Center for Justice. Website. https://www.brennancenter.org/our-work/research-reports/citizens-united-explained

Littleton, Cynthia. (2018). Merger Mania: Comcast Eyes Fox as CBS Resists Shotgun Wedding With Viacom. Variety. Website. https://variety.com/2018/biz/features/merger-mania-comcast-fox-cbs-viacom-1202810628/

Longley, Robert. (2019). Current Political Campaign Contribution Limits. ThoughtCo. Website. https://www.thoughtco.com/current-political-campaign-contribution-limits-3322056

Macias, Amanda. (2019). Trump picks acting Pentagon chief and former Boeing executive Patrick Shanahan to become next Secretary of Defense. CNBC. Website. https://www.cnbc.com/2019/05/09/trump-picks-ex-boeing-exec-patrick-shanahan-to-be-secretary-of-defense.html

Massoglia, Anna. (2020). Dark money groups steering millions to super PACs in 2020 election. Center for Responsive Politics. Website. https://www.opensecrets.org/news/2020/02/dark-money-steers-millions-to-super-pacs-2020/

Mauldin, John. (2019). America Has a Monopoly Problem. Forbes. Website. https://www.forbes.com/sites/johnmauldin/2019/04/11/america-has-a-monopoly-problem/#573615b12972

Salinas, Sara. (2019). AT&T's merger with Time Warner will stand, after DOJ loses its appeal and drops the case. CNBC. Website. https://www.cnbc.com/2019/02/26/appeals-court-upholds-decision-allowing-att-to-buy-time-warner.html

Semuels, Alana. (2019). 'They're Trying to Wipe Us Off the Map': Small American Farmers Are Nearing Extinction. Time. Website. https://time.com/5736789/small-american-farmers-debt-crisis-extinction/

Tyko, Kelly. (2019). Retailers Lost in the Last Decade: Toys R Us, Sports Authority, Blockbuster, Borders and Payless. USA Today. Website. https://www.usatoday.com/story/money/2019/12/29/decade-store-closings-biggest-retailers-lost-decade/2750954001/

Chapter 6:

ACLU. (2020). Surveillance Under the USA/Patriot Act. American Civil Liberties Union. Website. https://www.aclu.org/other/surveillance-under-usapatriot-act

ACLU. (2018). Stingray Tracking Devices: Who's Got Them? American Civil Liberties Union. Website. https://www.aclu.org/issues/privacy-technology/surveillance-technologies/stingray-tracking-devices-whos-got-them

Al-Othman, Hannah. (2016). WikiLeaks reveals 57,000 emails from the son-in-law of President Erdogan, 'proving his connection to ISIS operation smuggling oil into Turkey'. Daily Mail. Website. https://www.daily-mail.co.uk/news/article-4006568/WikiLeaks-reveals-57-000-emails-son-law-President-Erdogan-proving-connection-ISIS-operation-smuggling-oil-Turkey.html

Breitweiser, Kristen. (2016). WIKILEAKS: Kingdom of Saudi Arabia Funds and Logistically Supports ISIL. Huffpost. Website. https://www.huff-post.com/entry/wikileaks-kingdom-of-saud_b_12468758

Carafano, James et al. (2012). Fifty Terror Plots Foiled Since 9/11: The Homegrown Threat and the Long War on Terrorism. The Heritage Foundation. Website.

https://www.heritage.org/terrorism/report/fifty-terror-plots-foiled-911-the-homegrown-threat-and-the-long-war-terrorism

Clemons, Steve. (2014). 'Thank God for the Saudis': ISIS, Iraq and the Lessons of Blowback. The Atlantic. Website. https://www.theatlantic.com/international/archive/2014/06/isis-saudi-arabia-iraq-syria-bandar/373181/

CNN Wire Staff. (2012). Russia slams U.S. over sentence for arms dealer Viktor Bout. CNN. Website. https://www.cnn.com/2012/04/06/justice/russia-us-viktor-bout-case/index.html

Cray, Charlie. (2006). The 10 Most Brazen War Profiteers. Alternet. Website. https://www.alternet.org/2006/09/the_10_most_brazen_war_profiteers/

CRP. (2020). Lockheed Martin. Center for Responsive Politics. Website. https://www.opensecrets.org/orgs/lockheed-martin/lobbying?id=D000000104

Daly, John C.K. (2004). Viktor Bout. Jamestown Foundation Terrorism Monitor. Global Policy Forum. Website.

https://archive.globalpolicy.org/intljustice/wanted/2004/1021bout.htm

Dane, Lily. (2015). Blood Money: These Companies and People Make Billions of Dollars from War. Global Research. Website. https://www.globalresearch.ca/blood-money-these-companies-and-people-make-billions-of-dollars-from-war/5438657

Department of Defense. (2020). Iraq War Casualty Status Report. U.S. Department of Defense. Website. https://www.defense.gov/casualty.pdf

Devega, Chauncey. (2020). The tide is turning on Donald Trump: Former NATO supreme commander. Raw Story. Website. https://www.rawstory.com/2020/06/the-tide-is-turning-on-donald-trump-former-nato-supreme-commander/

Dickey, Christopher. (2017). VP Biden Apologizes for Telling Truth About Turkey, Saudi and ISIS. Daily Beast. Website. https://www.thedailybeast.com/vp-biden-apologizes-for-telling-truth-about-turkey-saudi-and-isis

Dobbs, Michael. (2002). US Had Key Role in Iraq Buildup. Washington Post. Global Policy Forum. Website. https://archive.globalpolicy.org/security/issues/iraq/saddam/2002/1230buildup.htm

Durden, Tyler. (2015). Secret Pentagon Report Reveals US "Created" ISIS As A "Tool" To Overthrow Syria's President Assad. LewRockwell.com. Website. https://www.lewrockwell.com/2015/05/tyler-durden/the-us-created-isis/

DW. (2003). Baghdad Shaken by 'Shock and Awe' Assault. Deutsche Welle. Website. https://www.dw.com/en/baghdad-shaken-by-shock-and-awe-assault/a-814725

Editors. (2020). September 11 Hijackers Fast Facts. CNN. Website. https://www.cnn.com/2013/07/27/us/september-11th-hijackers-fast-facts/index.html

Editors. (2011). Osama bin Laden killed by U.S. forces. History Channel. Website. https://www.history.com/this-day-in-history/osama-bin-laden-killed-by-u-s-forces

Editors. (2018). September 11 Attacks. History Channel. Website. https://www.history.com/topics/21st-century/9-11-attacks

Editors. (2017). Iran-Contra Affair. History Channel. Website. https://www.history.com/topics/1980s/iran-contra-affair

Editors. (2009). War in Iraq Begins. History Channel. Website. https://www.history.com/this-day-in-history/war-in-iraq-begins

Geller, Pamela. (2020). U.S. Reveals Key Islamic State Terror Money Provider Is In Turkey. https://gellerreport.com/2020/08/turkey-isis-funding.html/

Heilbrunn, Jacob. (2020). Why the United States Invaded Iraq. The New York Times. Website. https://www.nytimes.com/2020/07/28/books/review/to-start-a-war-robert-draper.html

Hendren, John. (2007). Missing Oil in Iraq Undercuts Progress. ABC News. Website. https://abcnews.go.com/WN/story?id=3168889&page=1

Hiro, Dilip. (2007). How Bush's Iraqi Oil Grab Went Awry. The Nation. Website. https://www.thenation.com/article/archive/how-bushs-iraqi-oil-grab-went-awry/

Intel.gov. (2015). Fact Sheet: Implementation of the USA Freedom Act of 2015. Office of the Director of National Intelligence. Website. https://www.intelligence.gov/index.php/ic-on-the-record-database/results/787-fact-sheet-implementation-of-the-usa-freedom-act-of-2015

Iraq Body Count. (2020). Iraq Body Count. Website. https://iraqbodycount.org/

Juhasz, Antonio. (2013). Why the war in Iraq was fought for Big Oil. CNN. Website. https://www.cnn.com/2013/03/19/opinion/iraq-war-oil-juhasz/index.html

Kadidal, Shayana. (2015). Surveillance After the USA Freedom Act: How Much Has Changed? Huffpost. Website. https://www.huffpost.com/entry/surveillance-after-the-us_b_8827952

Landau, Susan and Asaf Lubin. (2020). Examining the Anomalies, Explaining the Value: Should the USA FREEDOM Act's Metadata Program be Extended? Harvard National Security Journal. Vol. 11. Website. https://harvardnsj.org/wp-content/uploads/sites/13/2020/06/LANDAU_LUBIN_FINAL.pdf

Morgan, Andrew. (2013). The Patriot Act and Civil Liberties. Jurist. Website. https://www.jurist.org/archives/feature/the-patriot-act-and-civil-liberties/

Roberts, Adam. (2010). Lives and Statistics: Are 90% of War Victims Civilians? Survival, 52 (3), 115-136. Print.

Sale, Richard. (2003). Saddam Key in Early CIA Plot. United Press International. Global Policy Forum. Website.
https://archive.globalpolicy.org/security/issues/iraq/history/2003/0410saddam.htm

Samuels, Gabriel. (2016). Julian Assange: Isis and Clinton Foundation are both funded by Saudi Arabia and Qatar. Independent. Website.
https://www.independent.co.uk/news/people/julian-assange-clinton-foundation-isis-same-money-saudi-arabia-qatar-funding-a7397211.html

Sauter, Michael B. and Samuel Stebbins. (2017). Countries Buying the Most Weapons from the US Government. MSN. Website.
https://www.msn.com/en-us/money/markets/countries-buying-the-most-weapons-from-the-us-government/ar-AAnhTh3

Swan, Betsy Woodruff. (2020). DHS draft documents: White supremacists are greatest terror threat. Politico. Website.
https://www.politico.com/news/2020/09/04/white-supremacists-terror-threat-dhs-409236

Tyagi, Tal. (2019). The Iraq War Was Not About Oil. Quillette. Website.
https://quillette.com/2019/05/06/the-iraq-war-was-not-about-oil/

U.S. Senate. (1976). Report of the Senate Select Committee on Intelligence. Intelligence Activities and the Rights of Americans: Book II, Rept. 94-755, April 26, 1976, pp. 1-20. In Corporate and Governmental Deviance. Ed. M. David Ermann and Richard J. Lundmann.

Valori, Giancarlo. (2015). Turkey and the smuggling of ISIS oil. Modern Diplomacy. Website. https://moderndiplomacy.eu/2015/12/06/turkey-and-the-smuggling-of-isis-oil/

Walker et al. (2019). 10 Years. 180 school shootings. 356 victims. CNN. Website. https://www.cnn.com/interactive/2019/07/us/ten-years-of-school-shootings-trnd/

Whittaker, Zack. (2020). This is how police request customer data from Amazon. MSN. Website. https://www.msn.com/en-us/news/technology/this-is-how-police-request-customer-data-from-amazon/ar-BB19tcpa

Wilson, Chris. (2017). 41 Years of Mass Shootings in the U.S. in One Chart. TIME. Website. https://time.com/4965022/deadliest-mass-shooting-us-history/

Windrem, Robert. (2014). Who's Funding ISIS? Wealthy Gulf 'Angel Investors,' Officials Say. NBC. Website. https://www.nbcnews.com/storyline/isis-terror/who-s-funding-isis-wealthy-gulf-angel-investors-offi-cials-say-n208006

Woody, Christopher. (2020). Global Military Spending Rises, but US Still Outspends Everyone Else. Business Insider. Website. https://www.busi-nessinsider.com/global-military-spending-rises-but-us-still-outspends-everyone-else-2020-4#1-united-states-732-billion-up-53-from-2018-and-38-of-the-world-total-10

Woolf, Nicky. (2016). Stingray documents offer rare insight into police and FBI surveillance. The Guardian. Website. https://www.theguardian.com/us-news/2016/aug/26/stingray-oakland-police-fbi-surveillance

Young, Angelo. (2013). Cheney's Halliburton Made $39.5 Billion on Iraq War. International Business Times. Accessed on readersupportednews.org. Website. https://readersupportednews.org/news-section2/308-12/16561-focus-cheneys-halliburton-made-395-billion-on-iraq-war

Zero Hedge. (2015). Meet The Man Who Funds ISIS: Bilal Erdogan, The Son Of Turkey's President. Mint Press News. Website. https://www.mintpressnews.com/211624-2/211624/

Chapter 7:

Grim et al. (2014). Key Figures in CIA Crack-Cocaine Scandal Begin to Come Forward. Huffpost. Website. https://www.huffpost.com/entry/gary-webb-dark-alliance_n_5961748

Machiavelli, Niccolo. (2009). The Prince. Alma Classics Limited. CPI Group. Translated by J.G. Nichols. [Original: 1513; Il Principe].

Reinarman, C. and H. Levine. 2004. Crack in the rearview mirror: Decon-structing drug war mythology. Social Justice 31, 1-2.

Chapter 8:

Kelly, Cara. (2019). 13 sex trafficking statistics that explain the enormity of the global sex trade. USA Today. Website. https://www.usatoday.com/story/news/investigations/2019/07/29/12-trafficking-statistics-enormity-global-sex-trade/1755192001/

Muggah, Robert and Yves Tiberghien. (2018). The future global order will be managed by China and the US – get used to it. World Economic

Forum. https://www.weforum.org/agenda/2018/02/the-future-global-order-will-be-managed-by-china-and-the-us-get-used-to-it/

NCSL. (2016). Preventing Sex Trafficking and Strengthening Families Act of 2014. National Conference of State Legislatures. Website. https://www.ncsl.org/research/human-services/preventing-sex-trafficking-and-strengthening-families-act-of-2014.aspx